Knitting Vintage

Published in 2011by SevenOaks
An imprint of the Carlton Publishing Group
20 Mortimer Street
London W1T 3JW

10 9 8 7 6 5 4 3 2 1

A CIP catalogue record for this book is available from the British Library.

ISBN 978 1 86200 906 6

Printed and bound in Dubai

Senior Executive Editor: Lisa Dyer
Managing Art Director: Lucy Coley
Designer: Barbara Zuñiga
Copy Editors: Lara Maiklem and Camilla Davis
Production: Kate Pimm
Special Photography: Laura Knox
Stylist: Susan Downing
Hair and Makeup: Johanna Dalemo
and Janine Pritschow
Models: Katkin, Charlotte and Katie,
all at IMM models

Knitting Vintage

30 knitting projects inspired by period fashions

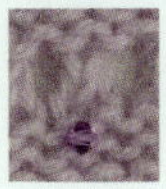

Claire Montgomerie

SevenOaks

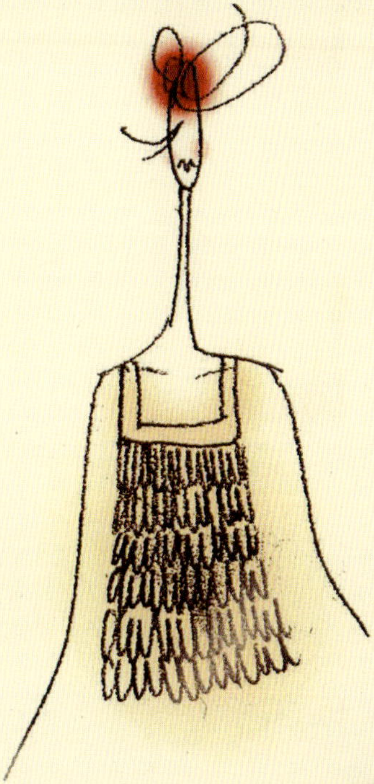

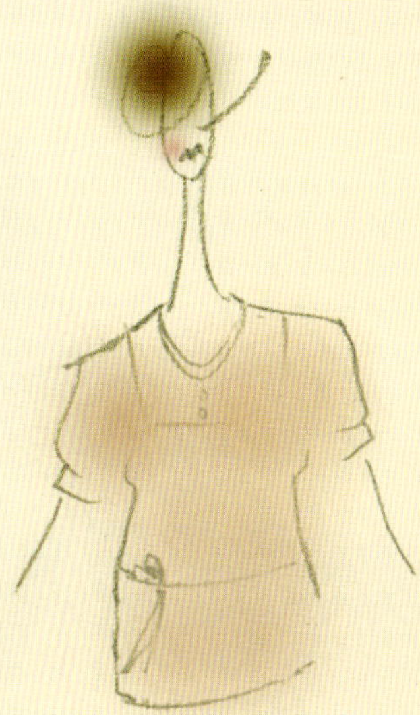

Contents

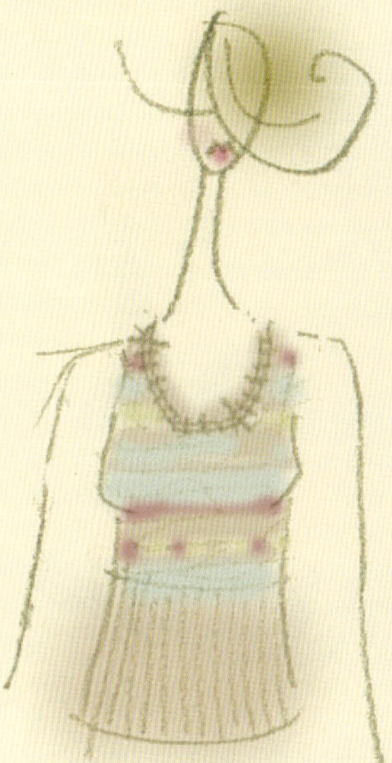

Introduction

The cyclical nature of fashion means that trends from the past will undoubtedly by recycled at some point in the future, and as a lover of all things retro, I am always glad to see a fresh and modern update of a past fashion, especially in knitwear. Using the extensive and colourful vintage pattern collection I have acquired over the years for inspiration, I have identified what I think are some of the most influential trends from the twentieth century and used these to design modern interpretations, so that today's knitter need not feel overwhelmed by the information, or lack of it, in an original pattern.

This book covers the time period between 1920, when women began to take up knitting as a viable way to make their own clothes as opposed to a hobby or a way to earn a living, and the 1980s, the last time when knitting was a strong force in fashion and a popular pastime. The 1990s saw the popularity of knitting and crafts wane, along with the rising popularity of streamlined and tailored fashion, a high street providing cheap and varied styles to suit all customers and a cash-rich, time-poor work force. It is only since the new millennium that a realization has dawned that the homogenization of fast fashion means it is nearly impossible to obtain individuality in dress. There has also been a turn towards sustainability within fashion and all areas of living, which has encouraged modern women to take time to relax and enjoy the benefits of an ancient craft while creating individual and unique garments.

As a passionate knitter I have found this full circle that we have turned in the last one hundred years incredibly pleasing, and it has been a delight to research and uncover the trends and progressions within the craft over this period and their indelible link to the changing social and economic climate. It is thrilling to me that such an ancient and traditional craft can still mean so much to modern women and can connect us to our ancestors in such a simple yet potent way.

I hope the book motivates you to make some of the garments, not just for dressing up for retro events but also for everyday wear, and also to search out your own vintage knitting patterns for inspiration.

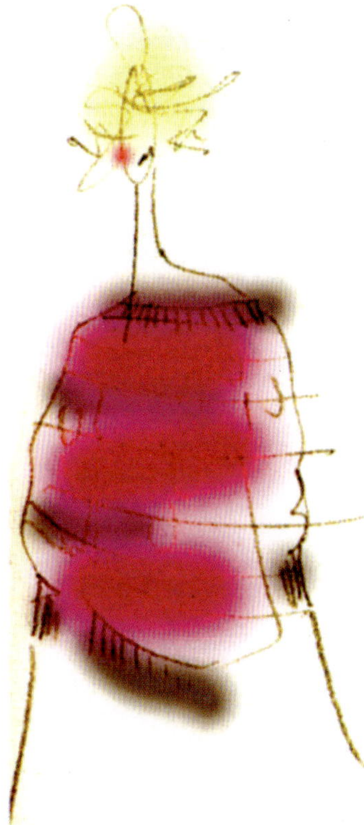

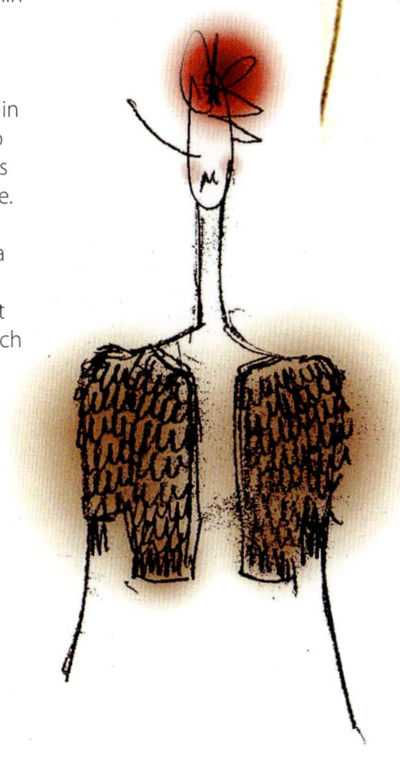

Knitting Past and Present

Knitting abbreviations as we know them today were taken up in the early 1900s, just before the period covered by this book. Therefore patterns from this era should be familiar and able to be used with relative ease to make garments today. Most of these vintage patterns tended to cater for the knitters of their time. In the past, knitting expertise was passed down through generations, mostly by word of mouth and demonstration, rather than by following a written pattern. In some communities, such as the more famous ones like Aran, in Ireland, where highly patterned cabled jumpers developed, and Fair Isle in Scotland, where a particular type of complicated colourwork was born, each family had its own traditional patterns or combinations of patterns. In the case of the knitted Gansey, handmade by fishermen or their wives as a protection from the harsh natural elements, the unique patterning worked into the sweater enabled seamen who lost their lives on the open waves to be identified.

This regional and intimate form of knitting produced incredibly proficient and skilled craftsmen and -women who were not often seen without their knitting. Although there are obviously parallels today, there is not the widespread level of ability there once was. Even women who did not knit frequently probably knew a basic sweater pattern by heart that they could then adapt for different family members or different occasions. As a whole, knitters were more accomplished, so they did not need incredibly detailed patterns to follow, and as a consequence, the patterns only contained the basics needed to work the pattern, with some sections omitted entirely as the maker was expected to draw upon prior knowledge of the craft. This, added to the fact that most of the yarns used do not exist anymore, means that the patterns can be confusing for modern crafters.

Vintage patterns also tend to only provide one size, partly due to the fact that most women would have known how to adapt the pattern to fit. Another problem with the sizing of the patterns is that the average woman's shape has changed throughout the years, especially around the bust and in height, so that the standard size given often does not fit the modern woman, with most patterns being far too short at the waist and on the arms.

Vintage knits, with a few tweaks, are still so wearable today, especially as there is a strong movement for dressing in vintage or retro style. As well as the literal reproductions of these patterns, there is room to make them less slavishly vintage in style. Fashion is cyclical, with the past influencing modern trends enormously, which means that by changing the body length, stitch pattern or even simply the colour, you can transform a dated pattern into a fresh, modern garment.

It has been interesting to note the changing trends, not only in fashion but also in the techniques, fibres and weights of yarn used in old knitting patterns. I have tried to retain some of the traditional techniques and processes where possible, while updating others. For example, some patterns have been made simpler, a quick knit for the modern woman who is short of free time. This is achieved by making patterns in thicker yarns or working the patterns in the round, a practice that was not widespread outside of a small number of places in continental Europe until relatively recently. I have also tried to include clever finishing, such as using grafting for seams, which, from what I can gather from my research, was also not as widespread in the past.

The breadth of yarns and fibre available to a knitter today is staggering by comparison. Natural yarns are making a huge comeback, so it is possible to use some beautiful wools and angoras, just like our predecessors would have done, but we can also benefit from much more advanced synthetic yarns and even from man-made/natural mixes, which combine the best of both worlds. Contemporary knitters really do have it all – the extensive vintage pattern back catalogue from the past from which to draw experience and inspiration and the fantastic selection of modern yarn to use for beautiful and durable garments.

Knitting Practicalities

For the purposes of this book, the reader is assumed to have a basic working knowledge of knitting, however, here is a brief summary of some of the most important considerations when you begin knitting. These include tips on yarn, needles and tension, as the right choice here will enable you to create a beautifully finished and accomplished garment with ease.

Types of Yarns

There are countless different types of yarn with various fibre content, weights and construction. Here is a quick guide to the properties of some of the most common, which should help you make an informed decision when choosing yarn for a project.

Acrylic Inexpensive, moth-resistant and easy to wash, acrylic is a great choice for beginners, but where possible choose a mix of acrylic and natural fibre (such as wool or angora) for the best drape and handle.

Alpaca The fleece from a South American camelid, alpaca is lustrous, silky and very warm, which makes it excellent for hats and scarves. It is, however, very heavy, so be careful when substituting this yarn for longer-length garments, as the resulting fabric tends to stretch under the weight.

Angora Super-soft, the hair of the angora rabbit is fluffy and glamorous.

Cashmere Considered the finest of the "noble" fibres, cashmere is soft, warm, fluffy and expensive. Choosing a cashmere–wool blend will give you many of the benefits of cashmere at a lower cost.

Cotton Useful for summer weights of garment, such as light sweaters, this plant fibre is readily available and inexpensive, but also has no stretch, so it can be more difficult to work and may highlight any irregularities in your stitching.

Mohair From the fleece of the angora goat, mohair is soft and seductive, but can be itchy when worn next to the skin.

Silk Light, lustrous and shiny, yet very strong, silk is a great choice for summer-weight garments and eveningwear.

Wool There is a vast variety of wool types, but all of them are easy to use, warm, elastic and usually give great stitch definition. Merino is the finest and softest sheep's wool.

Yarn Weights

Here is a general guide to the main categories. If you want to use a different yarn to the one stated in the pattern, and do not want to adapt the pattern at all, you must look for a yarn in a similar weight (or thickness) to the one stated, otherwise the knitting will give a different tension and the garment may come out the wrong size. To make matters even trickier, there are different terms for each category of weight; these differ between manufacturers and sometimes the weights are referred to as "plies". This can be confusing, as a "ply" refers to how many strands of the fibre are spun together to make the yarn; for example, some yarns comprised of two "plies" together result in a sportweight or "4-ply" thickness. It is always better to refer to the ball band for the tension/gauge of the yarn when knitted than to pay too much attention to what the manufacturer has named the yarn.

Laceweight/2-ply A very fine yarn used mainly to knit shawls and fine lace patterns, this is often knit on a slightly larger needle to accentuate the lace pattern.

Superfine/sock/3-ply/fingering A very thin yarn used for light, detailed and fine clothing, such as socks and the stockings, this weight was once a popular choice for all kinds of garments. Today a slightly thicker yarn is more commonly used for speed, which is why this category is hard to substitute in vintage patterns.

Fine/baby/4-ply/sport Commonly used for making light and delicate clothing for babies and children, this thin, useful yarn can also be used in adult garments to create a fine-gauge, lightweight fabric, perfect for layering and the changing seasons.

Light/double knitting (DK)/worsted This standard, practical weight of yarn is commonly used as a lightweight yet quick-to-knit choice, usually using a 3.75–4.5 mm (US 5–7) needle.

Medium/Aran/worsted Traditionally used in Aran sweaters, this has now become a modern favourite as it is perfect for accessories, such as scarves and hats, and works up quickly on a 5 mm (US 8) needle.

Bulky/chunky A thick yarn used to create chunky pieces, this knits up extremely quickly on larger needles yet it is not so bulky that the knitwear is hard to wear. Although not commonly used in the past, this weight has become more widespread due to its time-saving appeal to modern knitters.

Super bulky/roving The thickest and most cumbersome of yarns, this weight is most often used for accessories and interiors as the resulting garments can be heavy and extremely bulky. These yarns knit on needles in excess of a 10 mm (US 12) and were practically unheard of in the period looked at in this book, hence none of the projects use this weight.

Knitting Needles

In Europe, knitting needle size is metric in millimetres (mm) whereas in the US a separate system is in use (US size). International knitting magazines and books should give needle sizes in both millimetres and in US sizes. You will need all the knitting needles stated in the pattern if you knit to the tension given. Edges and hems are in general knitted on a smaller needle, and long edges may require a circular needle to fit all stitches.

There are many different types of needle, though metal ones are probably the most common. These are fast to knit with, as the stitches slip easily over the shaft, however, they do not have any flexibility and can be cold on the hands, which means that it can be more comfortable to knit with wooden or bamboo needles. These types grip the knitting more, but will bend as you knit, resulting in more flexibility and less stress on the hands and wrists. Plastic and casein needles are probably the least slippery, making them good choices for shiny, slippery yarns that need taming.

Double pointed and circular needles are used to work in the round to create seamless tubes, and double-pointed were more often used in the past than circulars, however circular needles are now becoming more popular.

Tension/Gauge

Essential in order to achieve the right size of garment, a tension swatch is used to ensure you are knitting at the tension called for in the pattern. To create a swatch, knit a small 10 cm (4 in) square in the main yarn and stitch used in the pattern, then count and calculate the average number of stitches per cm (in). Cast on a few more stitches and work more rows than the tension in the pattern suggests. This way a true tension is achieved within the square, as the edge stitches can often get distorted. When you have completed the swatch, use a measuring tape or ruler to take average measurements – count how many stitches and rows to 10 cm (4 in) at different points over the swatch.

Don't worry if your tension is not correct the first time, as knitting is not a precise art and everybody tends to knit at a different tension; in fact, gauge varies from knitter to knitter and also when different stitch combinations, yarn fibres and needle material are used and when knitting in the round.

If you find you have more stitches per cm (in) than indicated in the pattern, then your tension is too tight and you need to knit more loosely. The best way to do this is to increase the size of needle you use by a ¼ or ½ mm until the tension is as close as you can get it. If there are fewer stitches than required, then you are knitting too loosely, and you need to decrease the size of needle used in the same way.

Once you have the correct amount of stitches per cm (in), you will find that the garment will knit up to the correct size. Of course, knitting a tension swatch takes time, and with some small projects where a good fit is not required, you need not complete a swatch unless you really want to ensure the size.

Blocking

It is amazing how much can be achieved to neaten your finished knitting with simple blocking techniques. You must always block or steam your knitting before you sew it up to ensure all the pieces are the correct size and none will buckle. For simple garments, you can get away with simply pinning the pieces to shape and then lightly steaming to set the stitches. However, with lace – or with any piece that has been knitted to the wrong measurements for some reason – you must block the pieces carefully. Specialist blocking wires are available that are especially good for large lace pieces such as shawls or scarves. The same effect can be achieved by teasing your knitting gently to shape and pinning with blocking or marking pins to your ironing board (or, if not big enough, a large blanket or towel laid flat on the floor).

Once pinned, lay a very slightly damp towel or cloth on top of the knitting and iron gently. Be careful not to press firmly with the iron as you do not wish to flatten the naturally airy knitted stitches, only to let the heat and steam set the stitches into shape. Once the whole piece is warmed and steamed thoroughly, leave to cool down and dry. You can then unpin and remove the pieces.

Joining and Finishing

The finishing of a garment is often something that knitters most dislike to do, as good finishing is not even noticed when the garment is complete, but bad finishing is glaringly obvious.

When sewing up knitted pieces, try to keep the joins as invisible as possible. Always place the pieces next to each other on a flat surface with right sides facing and, if you wish, you may place markers at intervals up the edge to ensure you are sewing up evenly. Use a very neat mattress stitch to connect the edges, being sure to use the same colour of yarn as in the main body so that when the seams are pulled and moved when worn, the joining yarn cannot be seen.

Never cut the loose ends of yarn left at the edges of your knitting less than 10–20 cm (4–8 in) long, as these can slip through the loops of the stitches easily and unravel. However, these ends do need to be tidied, and you can do this by threading the ends in and out of the stitches on the reverse side of the work in any way that makes the length become invisible – such as by hooking through with a small crochet hook or darning in and out using a large darning or knitter's needle.

Abbreviations

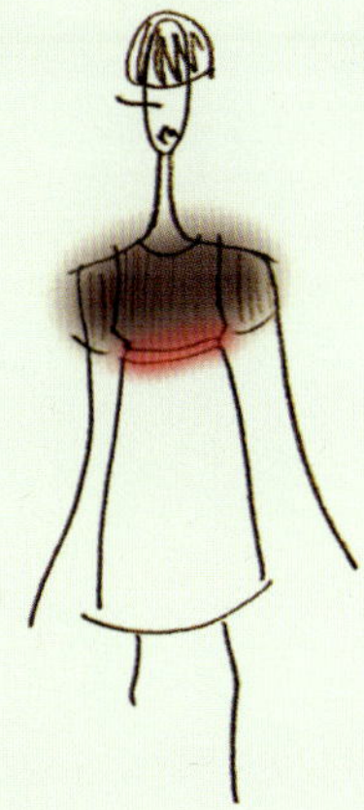

alt	alternate
beg	beginning
BO	bind off
cc	contrasting colour
ch	chain
cont	continue
cn	cable needle
CO	cast on
cont	continu(e) (ed) (es) (ing)
dec	decrease
DK	double knitting (yarn weight)
dpn	double pointed needle
F&B	front and back
foll	following
fwd	forward
inc	increase by knitting into front and back of stitch
k	knit
LHN/RHN	left hand needle/right hand needle
m1	increase by picking up bar between stitches
mc	main colour
p	purl
patt	pattern
PM	place marker
psso	pass slipped stitch over
pu	pick up
rem	remaining
rep	repeat
rev st st	reverse stocking stitch
rnd (s)	round(s)
RS(F)	right side (facing)
sc	single crochet
sl	slip
ssk	slip next st knit-wise
st(s)	stitch(es)
st st	stockinette (stocking) st
tbl	through back loop
tog	together
W&T	wrap and turn
WS(F)	wrong side (facing)
yo	yarn over

The Roaring Twenties

While it's fair to say that short bobbed hair and the "flapper girl" style are probably the most recognizable, almost clichéd, looks of the 1920s, informal and easy-to-wear knits were just as liberating for the women of the period as the new knee-length skirts. The straight-line chemise worn with a close-fitting cloche hat became the standard daytime uniform, and women's sportswear followed the boyish look with long cardigans for golf and sleeveless tops for tennis. The knitting patterns on the following pages explore the iconic, usually non-knitted styles of the age – such as the fringed flapper dress and ubiquitous string of beads – as well the trend for sporty beachwear and casual clothes.

Knitting and Fashion

Right up until the Victorian age, knitting was seen as a hobby and most knitted or crocheted items were products for the home such as doilies, tablemats and chair-back covers. Although the Victorians were partial to a lacy knit shawl or sometimes stockings, this was mainly where hand-knitted fashion began and ended. However, the 1920s saw knitted garments fall into fashion with the abandonment of corsets and restrictive clothing after the First World War. The war had made comfortable, simple and practical clothing a necessity. Suddenly, fashions were much easier to reproduce at home, rather than at the dressmaker's, which meant that high fashion became attainable to the masses. This was also true with knitwear.

Below: In this 1927 fashion illustration from *The Sphere*, elegantly dressed women are waiting to board a Pullman train. Art Deco stripes and chevrons decorate the drop-waisted knitted jersey suit.

Coco Chanel was a huge influence on reviving knitwear within fashion in the late 1910s and the 1920s. She took the luxury fibre cashmere from underwear to the catwalks, as well as using fluid knitted jersey fabrics, due to their low cost, which at the time seemed shocking in their structure. Chanel was breaking new ground in every way in fashion in the 1920s, creating one of the first partnerships with an avant-garde artist, Diaghilev, designing knitted bathing suits for his *Le Train Bleu* in 1924. These bathing suits were adapted into the mainstream and knitted swimwear remained popular well into the 1960s and 1970s, with many people over the age of 40 today probably able to recall the impracticality of the waterlogged bathing costumes of their childhood! Jean Patou, too, designed swimwear and sports ensembles with stripes and geometrics, perfect for the French Riviera, a favoured destination for the rich and beautiful. Home-knitting reflected the trend, with many patterns for long-line boyish swimsuits, sweaters and cardigans popular. These mainly used simple garter and stocking stitches to match the easy silhouette of the garment, sometimes with Art Deco-inspired patterning formed by block coloured intarsia.

Key themes

With the demise of the corset, the new "flapper" silhouette was long, lean and tubular – a shape well suited to knitting. By 1925 the waistline had dropped to below the hip and by 1927 it had disappeared completely. For daywear, the Bright

Young Things wore three-piece jersey dresses or cardigans and pleated skirts. For eveningwear they wore heavily embellished gowns with scalloped or assymetrical hemlines; short, sleeveless, and sometimes backless, the dresses exposed more skin than ever before. Innovative seaming, draping, gauzy fabrics, beads, sequins, fringing and feathers were all employed. Surface decoration took the form of Art Deco chevrons, stripes and other geometrics. Jeanne Lanvin and Edward Molyneaux embraced the look of the time, with elaborate embroidery, trimmings and bead-work – Lanvin working in light, clear floral colours while Molyneaux used a palette of neutrals.

Partly in reaction to the exuberant colours of the Ballet Russes and the multicoloured designs of Paul Poiret's "exotics" colours of golds, blue-greens, fiery reds and oranges in previous years, the 1920s produced a more subtle palette. Black and white became staples that would continue in fashion until the present day, while beige and ivory, accented with metallics and neutrals, were combined with cool shades.

The technological development of new fabrics and closures in clothing were affecting fashions of the 1920s, too. Natural fabrics, such as cotton and wool, were abundant in the decade, but rayon – "artificial silk" – became an important commodity as silk was in limited supply, as did leather. Zips, snaps and hooks and eyes were beginning to replace traditional lacings and buttons, even in knitted clothing.

Left: Knitted turbans, toques and skullcaps were all reinvented by designers in the 1920s as a necessary adjunct to an outfit. The close-fitting cloche hat, only possible to wear with the new short, flat bobs, was pulled low on the forehead. By 1928 the asymmetrical brim disappeared entirely.

The Roaring Twenties Mood Board

Inspiration for the cloche hat, fringed flapper top and Breton-style nautical jumper on the following pages comes directly from the Jazz Age flapper – free, young and spirited. Beads, pearls, feathers, flowers and Art Deco buttons can all be used for decoration on knitted pieces. The striped jumper captures the summer resort feel of the French Riviera, when everyone wore unisex fishermen's striped shirts, cotton trousers and espadrilles.

MALAGA
GRENET

Fringed Flapper Top

The image that comes to mind when thinking of the young flapper girl in the 1920s, dancing the Charleston and having a jolly old time, is with a long string of beads, a cocktail in hand and a shiny, fringed dress swinging in time with the music. This top is a modern and wearable version of those dresses, and can be dressed up for evenings and down for summer garden parties.

YARN

8[9:9:10] x 50 g (2 oz) balls of Gedifra Amara, 80% cotton, 20% polyamide, 100 m (109 yds) in shade 3721, peach

Alternative yarns: any DK or Aran/worsted weight yarn with a good drape will suit this project. Try tape or fancy yarns in cottons, viscose and silk for a looped fringe with a silky sheen and fabulous swing.

MEASUREMENTS

Actual chest

84	89	93	99 cm
33	35	36½	39 in

Length

34	36	37	38 cm
13¼	14	14½	14¾ in

TENSION/GAUGE

18 sts and 24 rows to 10 cm (4 in) in st st using 4.5 mm (US 7) circular knitting needles.

Left: This striking top can be accessorized simply with strings of pearls in the 1920s style, yet could equally be worn in a casual and thoroughly modern way with a pair of jeans and no extra embellishment.

NOTIONS

3.75 mm (US 5) circular knitting needles, 60 cm (24 in) long
4.5 mm (US 7) circular knitting needles, 60 cm (24 in) long
3.5 mm (US E) crochet hook
Darning needle

SPECIAL INSTRUCTIONS

All ribs are 1x1 unless otherwise stated.

Make Loop (ML):
Insert needle into next st without knitting it, slip two fingers from the left hand to the back of the knitting (take the yarn round over RHN in opposite direction to knitting, then around fingers of left hand to approx 12 cm (4¾ in) long) twice, then around needle again. Draw through 3 strands on RHN through st on LHN, slipping off original st. Put 3 loops back onto LHN and knit them together as 1 st. Loops are made on the back of the work.

For the purpose of this pattern, the reverse st st is the RS of the fabric.

Left: When creating the loops, ensure each is the same length for a sharp, layered look. Alternatively, vary the length for a textured fabric.

PATTERN

Using the 3.75 mm (US 5) circular needles, cast on 152 [160:168:178] sts and join for working in rnd, PM at beginning of the rnd and slip the marker at the beginning of every rnd.

Work 4 cm (1½ in) rib.

Change to 4.5 mm (US 7) circular knitting needles and st st and work until the piece measures 6 [8:9:10] cm (2¼ [3:3½:4] in) from cast-on edge.

Next rnd: ML into each st to end of rnd, making loops of approx 12 cm (4¾ in) long, or desired length.

Work straight in st st until the piece measures approx 14 [16:17:18] cm (5½ [6¼:6½:7] in) from cast-on edge.

Next rnd: ML into each st to end of rnd, making loops of approx 12 cm (4¾ in) long, or desired length.

Work straight in st st until the piece measures 22[24:25:26] cm (8½[9½:9¾:10¼] in) from cast-on edge.

Next rnd: ML into each st to end of rnd, making loops of approx 12 cm (4¾ in) long, or desired length. Work straight in st st until piece measures 30 [32:33:34] cm (11¾ [12½:13:13¼] in) from cast-on edge.

Next rnd: ML into each st to end of rnd, making loops of approx 12 cm (4¾ in) long, or desired length.

Change to 3.75 mm (US 5) circular knitting needles and work 4 cm (1½ in) rib. Cast off all sts loosely in patt.

Weave in all ends. Turn work inside out to RS and tidy each looped row by pulling each set of loops gently.

Straps

Using a 3.5 mm (US E) hook, chain 2 lengths of approx 25 cm (10 in).

Mark cast-off edge of the piece, approx 5 cm (2 in) in from the left side when laid flat; sew one end of one strap to the front at this point and the other end to the back. Repeat with rem strap, approx 5 cm (2 in) from the right side of the piece.

Above: To guarantee the loops remain secure and even, when the fabric is complete, neaten each row of loops by pulling lightly to tighten.

Above: The loops are made and held to the reverse of the work as they are knitted, therefore what is usually considered the reverse of the fabric becomes the right side.

String of Beads

A 1920s flapper girl always seemed to complete her outfit with an extra-long string of beads or pearls. These knitted beads are fun and colourful and can be made as long or short as you wish. The hues are a version of the strong period colour theme of neutrals mixed with brighter shades.

YARNS

50g (2 oz) of BC Garn Silkbloom, 55% merino, 45% mulberry silk, 140 m (153 yd) in small amounts of shade 14, grey (yarn A); shade 16, teal (yarn B); shade 20, violet (yarn C); and shade 21, lime green (yarn D).

Alternative yarns: Any yarn will do here, as the beads will just come out in differing sizes. This is a perfect project to use up scraps of yarn, as each bead uses minimal amounts and you could even use a different yarn for each bead.

MEASUREMENTS

One size. Necklace measures 150 cm (59 in) in length. Each bead measures approximately 1.5 cm (5/8 in) in diameter.

TENSION/GAUGE

Tension is not necessary, but ensure you knit tightly to keep the stitches from becoming loose and allowing the stuffing to show through.

Left: These beads are deceptively simple – and addictive! – to make. You can wear them in many different ways, including in layers piled on top of each other, knotted and wrapped around several times or twisted at the front.

NOTIONS

Pair of 3.25 mm (US 3) knitting needles
3.25 mm (size D) crochet hook
Darning needle
Toy stuffing

PATTERN

Using yarn A and the 3.25 mm (size D) hook, crochet a length of chain 150 cm (59 in) or to your desired length.

Using any yarn and 3.25 mm (US 3) needles, cast on 10 sts and k 8 rows; do not cast off these sts.

Break yarn and thread through rem sts, gathering all sts into a ring.

Sew up the side seam using mattress stitch, then stuff bead to desired fullness with toy stuffing. Run thread all round cast-on edge of bead and pull up tightly to close bead, ensuring stuffing does not show.

Make 50 beads, or desired amount, and thread onto the crocheted chain, through the holes at gathered ends. Sew the chain into a loop and weave in ends neatly.

Left: Here the beads are randomly spaced in odd groupings but for a different look thread them more densely along the length.

Lime Cloche Hat

When people think of fashions in the 1920s, they often think of the short, severe bob with a cute cloche hat atop. This knitted version, worked in a bright, modern shade, is softer and asymmetric to make it interestingly retro, contemporary and wearable.

Far left: A pretty cloche can be worn alone or with a vintage-style corsage pinned to the brim.

YARN

1 x 50 g (2 oz) ball of Karabella Boise, 50% cashmere, 50% superfine merino wool, 150 m (163 yd) in shade 69, lime

Alternative yarns: Any light DK or sportweight yarn is perfect. You may want to try knitting the hat on slightly larger needles in a pure wool yarn and then lightly felting it for a more authentically 1920s look. If you decide to do this, make sure you do tension swatches, then felt them to ensure it will not shrink too much.

MEASUREMENTS

One size, to fit the average adult head, approximately 56 cm (22 in) in circumference.

TENSION/GAUGE

26 sts and 30 rows to 10 cm (4 in) in st st using 3.25 mm (US 3) circular knitting needles.

NOTIONS

Pair of 3.25 mm (US 3) circular knitting needles, 40 cm (24 in) long
Pair of 3 mm (US 2.5) circular knitting needles, 40 cm (24 in) long
Set of 3.25 mm (US 3) double-pointed knitting needles
Stitch marker
Darning needle
Flower corsage (optional)

Far right: The quirky asymmetric brim is worked using short rows, as opposed to in the round like the crown. Practise the technique of wrapping stitches to prevent holes or gapping.

SPECIAL INSTRUCTIONS

Work as one piece, in the rnd throughout until the brim shaping. Start at the crown.

Using a set of four 3.25 mm (US 3) dpns, cast on 8 sts, distribute the stitches over the needles and position the needles for working in the rnd. PM at the beginning of the rnd and slip the marker at the beginning of every rnd.

Change to 40 cm (24 in) circular knitting needles when enough stitches, if desired.

At short row shaping for brim flap, wrap stitches to prevent holes.

PATTERN

Using 3.25 mm (US 3) dpns, cast on 8 sts.
Rnd 1: inc into every st by knitting twice into each st. (*16 sts*).
Rnd 2 (and every other rnd): k.
Rnd 3: [k2, yo] to end of rnd. *24 sts.*
Rnd 5: [k3, yo] to end of rnd. *32 sts.*
Rnd 7: [k4, yo] to end of rnd. *40 sts.*
Rnd 9: [k5, yo] to end of rnd. *48 sts.*

Cont in this way, increasing 8 sts each rnd by working one more st in between eyelet increases until there are 120 sts.

Work straight in st st without increasing for a further 8 cm (3¼ in).

Change to smaller circular knitting needles and work in 1x1 rib for 3 cm (1¼ in).

Brim

Change back to larger circular knitting needles and work in garter st for 2 rnds straight. [k1 rnd, p1 rnd].
Rnd 3: [k15, yo] to end of rnd. *128 sts.*
Next (and every other rnd): p (for garter st).
Rnd 5: [k16, yo] to end of rnd. *136 sts.*
Rnd 7: [k17, yo] to end of rnd. *144 sts.*
Rnd 8: p (for garter st).
Next row: k108, turn, leaving rem 36 sts unworked.
Next row: k72, turn, leaving rem 36 sts unworked.

Ear Flap

Work on 72 sts straight in short rows for ear flap as follows:
Next row: k68, turn.
Next row: k64, turn.
Cont in this way, working 4 less sts across each row until you are working over 40 sts, ending with a WSR.

Next row: k21, turn.
Next row: k2, turn.
Next row: k4, turn.
Next row: k6, turn.
Cont in this way, working 2 more sts each row until the row 'k36, turn' has been worked.

Next row: k39, turn, ending with a WSR. k to end of row, working over all 40 sts.

Rejoin for working in the rnd.
Work 4 rnd straight in garter st, over all sts. Cast off all sts loosely.

Weave in ends and pull in and secure hole at top of crown.

Breton-Style Nautical Jumper

This Breton-inspired jumper has taken inspiration from beachwear and the horizontal stripes were very à la mode at the time. The overall mood captures the summer resort feel of the French Riviera, a time when sunbathing, thanks to Coco Chanel, became fashionable. Traditionally it is said that the fisherman's striped shirt would allow a man to be spotted more easily if he had fallen into the sea. A classic standard that makes an appearance in nearly every spring/summer fashion collection, the stripy jumper can be worn with sailor-style wide-legged white or navy trousers for a timeless nautical feel or paired with a white denim skirt and wide navy-style belt.

YARNS

3[3:4] x 100 g (4 oz) balls each of Berroco Ultra Alpaca 50% superfine alpaca, 50% Peruvian wool, 198 m (215 yds) in shade 6298, admiral mix (yarn A) and shade 6201, winter white (yarn B).

Alternative yarns: any Aran or worsted weight yarn. Alternatively, try cotton for a summery beach feel.

MEASUREMENTS

Bust

81–86	91–97	102–107 cm
32–34	36–38	40–42 in

Actual Size

91	101	111 cm
36	39¾	43¾ in

Length from Shoulder

53	55	56 cm
20¾	21½	22 in

Sleeve Seam

23	23	23 cm
9	9	9 in

TENSION/GAUGE

20 sts and 26 rows to 10 cm (4 in) in st st using 5 mm (US 8) knitting needles.

NOTIONS

Pair of 4.5 mm (US 7) knitting needles
Pair of 5 mm (US 8) knitting needles
4 mm (US G) crochet hook (for button loops)
3 buttons, approx 1.5 cm (5/8 in) in diameter
Darning needle

PATTERN

Back and Front Alike

Using 4.5 mm (US 7) knitting needles and yarn A, cast on 81[91:101] sts and work 10 cm (4 in) in 1x1 rib as folls:

Row 1(RS): k2, *p1, k1, rep from * to last st, k1.

Row 2: p2, *k1, p1, rep from * to last st, p1.

Rep last 2 rows for length of rib, ending with a row 2 increasing 12 sts evenly along last row. *93[103:113] sts.*

Change to yarn B and 5 mm (US 8) knitting needles and work in st st beg with a k row for 8 rows.

Far left: Wear this sweater in nautical style with drawstring pants and white plimsolls, or dress it up with a skirt and heels for an added elegance to match the vintage buttons at the shoulder.

Below: If the nautical look is not for you, try working the stripes in bright, contrasting shades for a striking design.

Change to yarn A and work 8 rows. Cont in st st in alternate stripes of each colour as established until the work measures approx 34 cm (13¼ in) from cast-on edge, ending with 8 rows in yarn A.

Armholes

Cast off 7[8:9] sts at beg of next 2 rows, then dec 1 st at both ends of every row 4[5:6] times, then every foll alt row 4 times. *63[69:75] sts.*

Work straight in st st continuing in stripes until you reach 3rd yarn B stripe from armhole shaping, then cont in yarn A until the work measures approx 15[17:18] cm (6[6½:7] in) from beg of armhole shaping, ending with a p row.

If necessary, change to yarn A and work yoke as folls:
Row 1: k1, *p1, k1, rep from * to end.
Rep row 1 until work measures 19[21:22] cm (7½[8¼:8½] in) from armhole shaping, ending with a WSR.

Shoulders

Cast off 6 sts at beg of next 4 rows and then 5[6:6] sts at beg of next 2 rows. Cast off rem 29[33:39] sts loosely in pattern.

Sleeves

Using 4.5 mm (US 7) knitting needles and yarn A, cast on 51[55:59] sts and work 5 cm (2 in) in 1x1 rib as folls:
Row 1(RS): k2, *p1, k1, rep from * to last st, k1.
Row 2: p2, *k1, p1, rep from * to last st, p1.

Rep last 2 rows for length of rib, ending with a row 2, increasing evenly along last row to 73[77:81] sts.

Change to yarn B and 5 mm (US 8) knitting needles and work in st st beg with a k row for 8 rows.

Below: The type of button used at the shoulder can change the entire style of this jumper. Here, vintage pearlized buttons create a sophisticated and nostalgic feel.

Change to yarn A and work 8 rows. Cont in st st in alternate stripes of each colour as established until the work measures approx 23 cm (9 in) from cast-on edge, ending 8 rows in yarn A.

Shape Top

Cast off 7[8:9] sts at beg of next 2 rows, then dec 1 st at both ends of foll 3 rows. *53[55:57] sts.*

Dec 1st st both ends of every foll 4th row to 29[31:33]sts. Cont in stripe sequence until you reach 3rd yarn B stripe from armhole shaping, then cont in yarn A for rem of sleeve.

Cast off, taking 3 sts together at a time until last 2[4:3] sts; cast these sts off together.

Finishing

Block all pieces lightly.

Sew together right shoulder seam, then left shoulder seam from armhole edge to 2 cm (¾ in).

Set in sleeves and then sew up side and arm seams.

Sew 3 buttons along front left shoulder, approx 1 cm (½ in) from edge.

Using 4mm (US 9) crochet hook and yarn B, crochet 3 x 2 cm (¾ in) loops and attach to reverse edge of left shoulder back seam, corresponding to button placement.

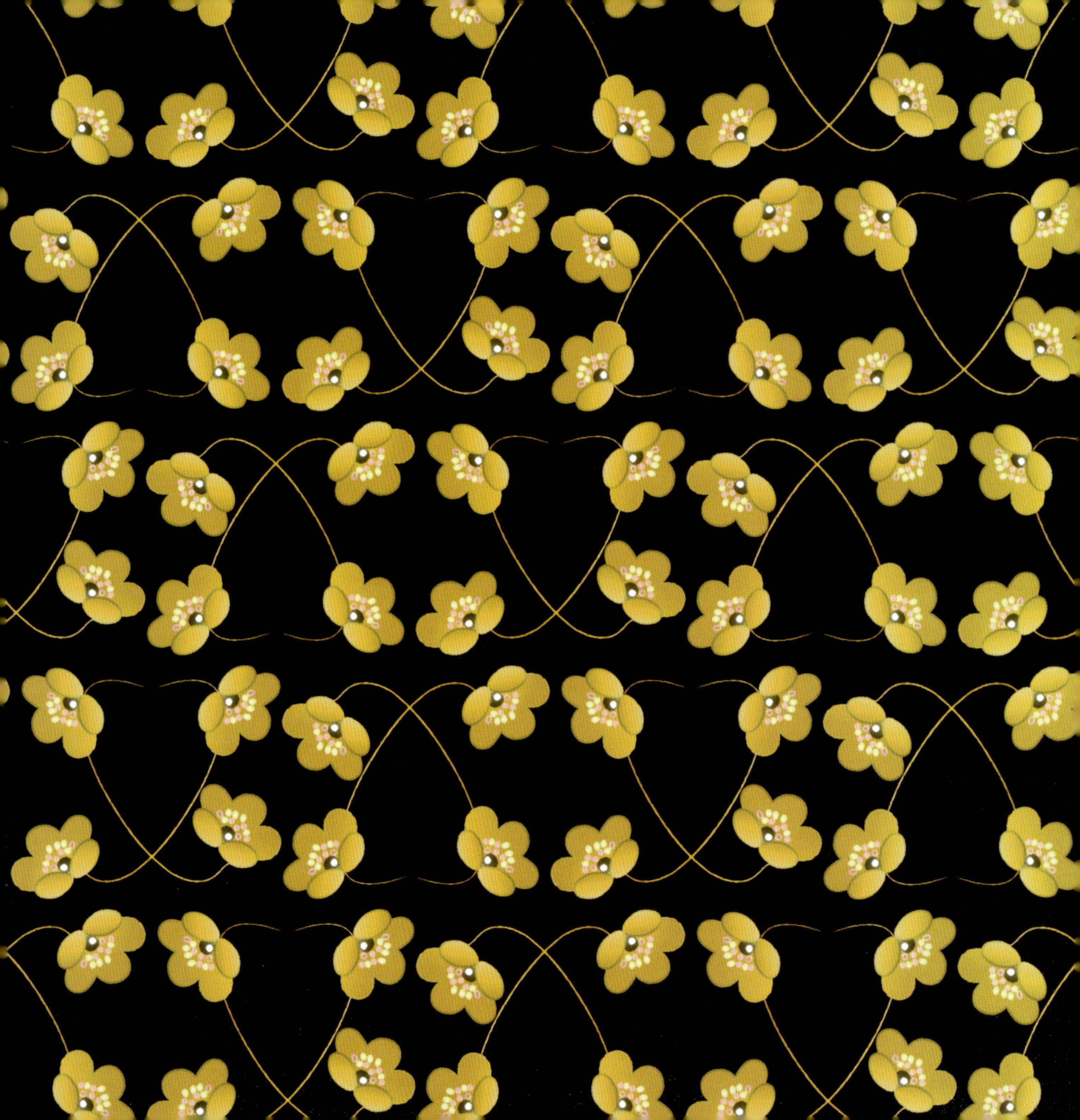

The Glamorous Thirties

The 1930s saw a very different look develop in fashion. The style was far more feminine than the boyish flapper of the 1920s, with nipped-in waists and an emphasis on the bust. This look translated to knitting, with darts and shaping used to create a curvier silhouette. With the Great Depression overshadowing this decade, and the Second World War starting in 1939, hand-knitting became more widespread as a matter of necessity. Women who could knit and sew created their own versions of the feminine and elegant clothes that the era demanded, despite the hardships. Thirties' ideas, such as the bolero jacket and silk blouse, are translated into knitwear patterns on the following pages, but traditional items, such as the classic Fair Isle jumper, here in a low-necked, sleeveless vest form, and the knitted beret, are also included.

Knitting and Fashion

The 1930s were the Golden Age of Hollywood, and the movies influenced everyday life. Women wanted to be as beautiful and stylish as the actresses they saw on the big screen, and they achieved this by making their own clothes. With movie stars such as Katharine Hepburn wearing trousers on-screen and off, a relaxed, informal style was suddenly acceptable. This, combined with the growth in the sportswear industry and a preoccupation with physical fitness, meant fashion could be casual and comfortable.

The rise in popularity of hand-knitting was reflected by the release of the long-running and extremely popular *Vogue Knitting* and *Stitchcraft* pattern booklets in the early part of the decade. These booklets were a mine of information for the domestic goddesses of the age. Although they may seem to come from a less enlightened age, when women were expected to get married and care for a family rather than "have it all", they are filled with fantastic patterns and tips that are still relevant to the crafter of today.

Key themes

The Italian fashion designer Elsa Schiaparelli was huge at the time. In the late 1920s, she designed a knitted sweater with a *trompe l'oeil* bow around the neck that was copied throughout the early 1930s in knitting booklets such as *Stitchcraft*. Her bold use of colour inspired the palette of the age, with blushes and neutral shades highlighted by strong fuchsia, which she was the first to name "shocking pink", and jewel-like purples and emeralds. Schiaparelli also designed fantastically surreal and oddly shaped hats, inspired by the artists of the age. Knitting books of the 1930s are filled with fascinating

Right: The short boleros and shrugs, often in fur and worn over silk bias-cut dresses of the 1930s, provided the inspiration for the Loopy-Knit Bolero on page 42. Here a model wears a short white ermine jacket in 1931.

and sculptural headpieces perched atop extremely elegant hairstyles.

The trend for Fair Isle, begun by the Prince of Wales in the 1920s, was still going strong in the 1930s, with many rural knitters creating beautiful, almost couture, handcrafted pieces for the upper classes. Scandinavia, like Scotland, has a rich history of multicoloured knitting. The Great Depression took a particularly heavy toll on some Swedish communities, so to help support themselves local women in Bohuslän started the Bohus Stickning (Bohus knitting) industry. The sweaters they knitted were beautiful works of art, and the Bohus jumper or twinset soon became a must-have item for every well-heeled lady. The women of Bohuslän continued to knit sweaters for Bohus Stickning until the late 1960s ceased production. Meanwhile, those who could not afford the genuine article reproduced it themselves at home.

Knitwear was most prevalent in sportswear – taking the form of bathing suits, tennis dresses, golfing sweaters and skiwear – as the fibre provided lightweight warmth. In the USA, knitwear manufacturers were adept at marketing their products, with the swimwear companies Jantzen and Catalina actually starting out as knitting mills.

The 1930s also saw nightwear and underwear become as elegant as daywear. Bias-cut, silk nightgowns were topped with extravagant, yet cosy, knitted bed jackets, and underwear became lacy and fitted. Such pieces have been adapted in this chapter to create modern and stylish outerwear.

Above: Coco Chanel's knitted suit spawned thousands of imitators in the 1930s. In this image from a 1930s fashion magazine, designs of the time are shown – a rose-coloured knitted dress and a tweed-like cardigan suit in brown wool with a yellow and pink fleck, both by Jaegar; a cap and cravat in coral-coloured wool; and a blue, black and white geometric jumper with knitted blue wool gloves, both from Stonehenge Woollen Industry.

The Glamorous Thirties Mood Board

Schiaparelli's "shocking pink", the bias-cut dresses of Madeleine Vionnet, silky blouses with scarf-like jabots and the glamour of Hollywood movie stars have all provided inspiration for the patterns on the following pages. The decade was more about form and feminity than detail and decoration, so pure romantic colours and figure-hugging silhouettes are emphasized, with embellishment less important.

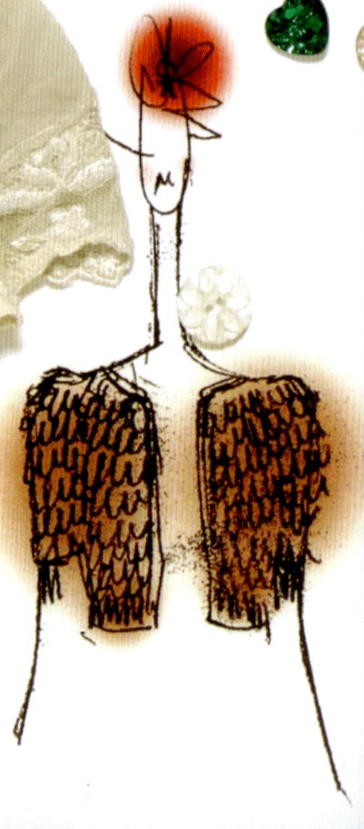

STITCHCRAFT
1939
6D
Gifts for
CHRISTMAS
SNAP

Knitted Silk Blouse

Far right: Styled with a timeless pencil skirt and chic clutch, the blouse imparts the glamour of the 1930s while still looking entirely relevant today.

Below: The intricate lace pattern of the fabric is simply stunning worked in a shimmering silk with heavy drape, although this handle could also be achieved with a bamboo yarn.

A woman could not call her wardrobe complete in the 1930s without a versatile silk blouse. This pretty sweater, though technically not a blouse as it does not button down, is a very wearable jersey for evening or can be worn more casually in the daytime to give everyday jeans a touch of glamour.

YARN

9[10:12] x 50 g (2 oz) balls of BC Garn Jaipur Silk, 100% mulberry silk, 125m (136 yds), in shade jm15.

Alternative yarns: any 4-ply to sport-weight yarn. Try to keep any substitute cool and with a beautiful drape, to allow for the illusion that the fabric is a silk weave.

MEASUREMENTS

Bust

81–86	91–97	102–107 cm
32–34	36–38	40–42 in

Actual Size

91	101	111 cm
35¾	39¾	43¾ in

Length from Shoulder

56	59	62 cm
22	23¼	24¼ in

Sleeve Seam

6	7	8 cm
2½	2¾	3¼ in

TENSION/GAUGE

22 sts and 30 rows to 10 cm (4 in) in st st using 3.75 mm (US 5) knitting needles.

24 sts and 32 rows to 10 cm (4 in) across lace patt using 3.5 mm (US 4) knitting needles.

NOTIONS

Pair of 3.25 mm (US 3) knitting needles
Pair of 3.5 mm (US 4) knitting needles
Pair of 3.75 mm (US 5) knitting needles
2 x 1.5 cm (5/8 in) diameter buttons
Darning needle

SPECIAL INSTRUCTIONS

Lace Stitch

Row 1(RS): k2, *k2tog, yfwd, sl 1, k1, psso, k2; rep from * to end of row.
Row 2: p3, *(p1, k1) into next st, p4; rep from * ending last rep p3 instead of p4.
Row 3: k1, *k2tog, yfwd, k2, yfwd, sl1, k1, psso; rep from * to last st, k1.
Row 4: p.
Row 5: k2, *yfwd, sl 1, k1, psso, k2tog, yfwd, k2, rep from * to end.
Row 6: p.
Row 7: k1, * sl 1, k into next st, leaving loop on LHN, psso, k2tog, by knitting loop on LHN together with next st, yfwd, sl 1, k into next st, leaving loop on LHN, psso, k2tog, by knitting loop on LHN together with next st; rep from * to last st, k1.

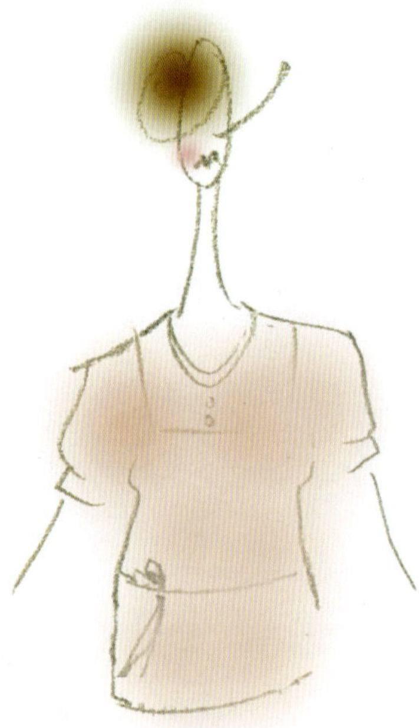

Right: A stocking stitch yoke provides a bold and interesting contrast to the open lace of the body, a fabulous feature that's easily achieved.

Row 8: p3, *(p1, k1) into next st, p4; rep from * ending last rep p3 instead of p4.
Row 9: k1, yfwd, *sl1, k1, psso, k2, k2tog, yfwd; rep from * to last st, k1.
Row 10: p6, *(p1, k1) into next st, p4; rep from * to last 2 sts, p2.
Row 11: k2, *yfwd, sl1, k1, psso, k2tog, yfwd, k2, rep from * to end.
Row 12: p.
Row 13: k1, *k2tog, yfwd, k2, yfwd, sl1, k1, psso; rep from * to last st, k1.
Row 14: p.
Row 15: k1, yfwd, *(sl1, k into next st, leaving loop on LHN, psso, k2tog, by knitting loop on LHN together with next st) twice, yfwd, rep from * to last st, k1.
Row 16: p6, *(p1, k1) into next st, p4; rep from * to last 2 sts, p2.
These 16 rows form patt, rep for lace pattern throughout.

PATTERN

Back

With 3.5 mm (US 4) needles, cast on 98 [110:122] sts and work lace pattern 4 times, then begin a 5th repeat, but end with a row 3.
Row 68 (inc row): p, inc in every 8th [9th:10th] st, 12 times, p2 (110 [122:134] sts, 2 complete patts inc).

Cont in patt, starting with a 5th row of lace patt, working straight until back measures 37[38:39] cm (14½[15:15½] in) ending with a WSR.

Shape Armholes and Shoulders

Cast off 6 sts at beg of next 4 rows (86[98:110] sts). Work straight in pattern until armhole measures 19[21:23] cm (7½[8¼:9] in).

Cast off 14 sts at beg of next 2 rows, then 12[8:10] sts at beg of next 2[4:4] rows, leave rem 34[38:42] sts on holder.

Front

Work as for back until armholes measure 5 cm (2 in), ending with a WSR. Divide for neck.
Next row: patt 14, turn, leaving rem sts on holder.
Cont straight in patt on these 14 sts until armhole measures 19[21:23] cm (7½ [8¼:9] in). Cast off all 14 sts.

Return to rem sts, slip centre 58[70:82] sts on holder, rejoin yarn to last 14 sts at neck edge and work to correspond with opposite side.

With RSF, join yarn to centre 58[70:82] sts and work 2 rows st st.

Next row: k 29[35:41], place next 29[35:41], sts on holder, cast on 3 sts for button tab, turn.
Cont on these 32[38:44] sts in st st, working 4 neck edge sts in garter st until yoke measures 11[13:15] cm

(4¼ [5:5¾] in) from armhole shaping, ending with a RSR.

Next row: cast off 16[17:18] sts, p to end. dec 1 st at neck edge of next row and 3[4:5] foll alt rows.
Cont straight until yoke measures same as left shoulder, ending with a p row.
Cast off 12[8:10] sts at beg of next row 0[1:1] foll alt rows.

Rejoin yarn to rem right yoke sts at neck edge, cast on 2 sts and k to end. Work in st st for 3[4:5] cm (1¼[1½:2] in) on these 31[37:43] sts, working 4 edge sts in garter st, ending with a WSR.

Make buttonhole: k2, yfwd, k2tog, k to end of row.

Cont in st st with garter edge sts, until work measures same as left yoke. Work neck and shoulder shaping to correspond with left side, reversing all shapings.

Sleeves

Using 3.25 mm (US 3) needles, cast on 63[67:71] sts and work 2.5 cm (1 in) in 1x1 rib.

Change to 3.75 mm (US 5) needles and work in st st, increasing evenly to 83 [87:91] sts on first row.
Work in st st until sleeve measures 6[7:8] cm (2½[2¾:3¼] in).

With RSF, shape top by casting off 6 sts at beg of next 4 rows, then dec 1 st at both ends of every foll alt row 3 times.

Work 15[16:17] cm (6[6¼:6¾] in) straight in st st. Cast off all rem sts, taking two sts each time to last st. Fasten off.

Finishing

Block all pieces lightly.

Join yoke and shoulder panels of front and sew button placket of left side down under right side.

Join shoulder seams.

Neck Band

Using 3.75 mm (US 5) needles, rejoin yarn to right front with RSF, pick up and knit 16[17:18] sts from centre front, 12 sts up right neck, knit 34[38:42] sts from holder at back, pick up 12 sts down left neck and 16[17:18] sts from left front 90[96:102] sts.
Work 3 rows garter st on these sts.
Next row: k2, yfwd, k2tog, k to end of row.
Work 2 further rows straight in garter st. Cast off all sts loosely.

Set-in sleeves, gathering all fullness to shoulder and sew up sleeve and side seams, leaving 10 cm (4 in) open at the bottom of the blouse.

Either make a cord of approx 1 m (1 yd) long using the main yarn, or use a length of ribbon to run in and out of the lace at waist, where increase row was made. Gather and tie in a bow.

Sew on buttons.

Below: A twisted cord highlights the shaping at the waist, but alternatively you could thread through a ribbon in a contrasting colour.

Right: For an evening look, wear this bolero with a bias-cut dress, as the well-heeled ladies of the 1930s would have done, or cosy up for everyday comfort and wear it with jeans and a vest.

Loopy-Knit Bolero

This decade saw glamour seep into every area of a woman's life, including the bedroom. There were many knitting patterns around for cosy yet sensational bed jackets to be worn over long satin nightdresses. This pattern is derived from the few that exist using the "loopy fur" stitch, which is fun to knit and to wear. Here, it becomes a very warm yet glamorous bolero, which these days needn't be confined to the bedroom. The bolero could be worn casually over jeans or even over a silky bias-cut dress, similar to the original nightgowns, as a dressy alternative.

YARN
13[14:16] x 50 g (2 oz) balls of GGH Wollywasch, 100% DK Wool, 125 m (137 yd) in shade 162

Alternative yarns: any DK weight yarn. Try a shiny, heavier yarn or even tape yarn of the same weight to change the drape and effect of the loops. Remember that the fur stitch eats yarn very quickly, so you will need a lot of yardage.

MEASUREMENTS

Bust

81–86	91–97	102–107 cm
32–34	36–38	40–42 in

Finished Bust

91	101	107 cm
36	40	42 in

Length from Shoulder

40	42	45 cm
15¾	16½	17¾ in

Sleeve Seam

25	26	27 cm
10	10¼	10½ in

Armhole

19	21	23 cm
7½	8¼	9 in

TENSION/GAUGE
20 sts and 24 rows to 10 cm (4 in) in loop st using 4 mm (US 6) knitting needles.

NOTIONS
Pair of 3.5 mm (US 4) knitting needles
Pair of 4 mm (US 6) knitting needles
Darning needle

SPECIAL INSTRUCTIONS
All ribs are 1x1 unless otherwise stated.

Loop Stitch
Make Loop (ML):
Insert needle into next st without knitting it, slip 2 fingers from left hand to back of knitting, [take yarn round over RHN in opposite direction to knitting, then around fingers of left hand to approx 3–4 cm (1¼–1½ in) long] twice, then around needle again.

Draw through 3 strands on RHN through st on LHN, slipping off original st. Put 3 loops back onto LHN and knit them together as 1 st.

Loops are made on the back of the work.

Below: The wool yarn holds the loops of this stitch incredibly well, causing the small, curling strands to stand up, creating a fabulously satisfying pile fabric. Keep the loops relatively short and even to maintain this effect.

Above: The ribbed edgings and cuffs pull the fabric close to the body, lending shape to the boxy garment and preventing it from becoming too bulky and shapeless.

Far right: When setting in the sleeve cap, ensure you gather all fullness towards the shoulder seams in neat pleats, to emphasize the strong shape of the ruching.

PATTERN

Back

Using 3.5 mm (US 4) needles, cast on 91[101:107] sts. Work 5 cm (2 in) in rib, ending with a RSR.

Change to 4 mm (US 6) knitting and work 2 rows garter st.
Next row: k2, ML into next and each st along row to last 2 sts, k2.
Work 3 rows garter stitch.
Work last 4 rows until work measures approx 21[21:22] cm (8¼[8¼:8¾] in), ending with a loop row.

Shape Armholes

Cast off 8[9:9] sts at beg of next 2 rows, then dec 1 st at both ends of next 2 rows and then foll 3 alt rows. *65[73:79] sts.*

Cont in patt, work straight until the work measures approx 19[21:23] cm (7½[8¼:9]in) from beg of armhole shaping, ending with a loop row.

Shape Shoulders

Cast off 7[7:8] sts at beg of next 2 rows, then 7[8:8] sts at beg of foll 4 rows. Cast off rem 23[27:31] sts.

Left Front

Using 3.5 mm (US 4) needles, cast on 45[49:53] sts. Work 5 cm (2 in) in rib, ending with a RSR.

Second size only:
Inc 1 st at beg of last row. *50 sts.*

Change to 4 mm (US 6) needles and work 2 rows garter st.
Next row: k2, ML into next and each st along row to last 2 sts, k2
Work 3 rows garter stitch.
Work last 4 rows until work measures same as back to armholes, ending with a WSR.

Shape Armhole

Cast off 8[9:9] sts at beg of next row, then dec 1 st at armhole of next 2 rows and then foll 3 alt rows. *32[36:39] sts.*

Cont in patt, work straight until the work measures approx 13[15:17] cm (5¼[6:6¾] in) from beg of armhole shaping, ending with a loop row.

Shape Neck

Cast off 5[6:8] sts, work to end. *27[30:31]sts.*
Dec 1 st at neck edge of next 3 rows, maintaining pattern, then dec 1 st at neck edge of every alt row until 21[23:24]sts rem.

Cont straight until work measures same as back, ending with a WSR.

Shape Shoulder

Cast off 7[7:8] sts at beg of next row, then 7[8:8] sts at beg of foll 2 alt rows.

Right Front

Complete as for left front, reversing all shaping.

Sleeves

Using 3.5 mm (US 4) needles, cast on 61[71:77] sts.
Work 5 cm (2 in) in 1x1 rib, ending with a RSR, increasing 6 sts evenly along last row. *67[77:83] sts.*

Change to 4 mm (US 6) needles and work 2 rows garter st.
Next row: k2, ML into next and each st along row to last 2 sts, k2.
Work 3 rows garter stitch.
Work last 4 rows until work measures approx 25[26:27] cm (10[10¼:10½] in), ending with a loop row.

Shape Sleeve Top

Cast off 8[9:9] sts at beg of next 2 rows, then dec 1 st at both ends of next 2 rows and then foll 3 alt rows. *41[49:55] sts.*

Work straight for a further 15 rows, ending on a k row.
k16[19:21], inc into each of next 9[11:13] sts, k to end.
Work a further 5 cm (2 in) straight.
Cast off all stitches.

Making Up

Sew together shoulder seams with a neat backstitch.

With RSF and using 3.5 mm (US 4) needles, pick up and k 24[26:26] sts up right neck, 23[27:31] sts across back neck and 24[26:26] sts down left neck. *71[77:83] sts.*

Work on these 71[79:83]sts in rib for 4 rows. Cast off all sts loosely in rib.

Set in sleeves, gathering all fullness in pleats, using a neat backstitch. Sew up side and sleeve seams.

Hollywood-Style Beret

The beret is relevant throughout the decades, but in the 1930s the Hollywood look was inevitably finished off with just such a hat, perched jauntily at an angle so that the perfectly styled hair can be seen underneath. Think Marlene Dietrich, who had a wardrobe full, including one by Elsa Schiaparelli. In a nod to this innovative designer, whose knitted intarsia, *trompe l'oeil* patterns are couture wonders, this beret is created in a colour similar to Schiaparelli's "shocking pink", which she launched in 1936 – an incredibly fresh, bold colour for the time.

YARNS

2 x 50 g (20 oz) balls of Blue Sky Alpacas Sportweight 100% baby alpaca, 10 m (110 yds) in shade 538, hibiscus (yarn A)

1 x 50 g (20 oz) ball of Blue Sky Alpacas Sportweight 100% baby alpaca, 10 m (110 yds) in shade 505, taupe (yarn B)

Alternative yarns: any sportweight or DK yarn; try merino wool for a lighter version that will not drape as much.

MEASUREMENTS

One size, to fit average adult head of up to approx 55 cm (21½ in).

TENSION/GAUGE

18 sts and 24 rows to 10 cm (4 in) in st st using 5.5 mm (US 8) knitting needles.

NOTIONS

3 mm (US 2), 40 cm (16 in) long circular knitting needles

5.5 mm (US 8), 40 cm (16 in) long circular knitting needles

Set of 5.5 mm (US 8) double-pointed needles

Stitch marker

Darning needle

SPECIAL INSTRUCTIONS

k3togtbl = knit 3 stitches together through back loops.

p2sso = pass 2 slipped stitches over.

On the crown change down to dpns when the sts are too few to reach around a circular needle.

PATTERN

Using 3 mm (US 2) needles and yarn A, cast on 104 sts and join for working in the rnd, PM at beg of round.

Work 12 rnds k1, p1 rib.

Next rnd: rib 2, *inc in next st, rib 1; rep from * to end of row. *(155 sts).*

Change to 5.5 mm (US 8) needles and work 16 rnds st st, then change to pattern for crown as folls:

Rnd 1: k2tog, (k5, yfwd, k1, yfwd, k5, sl1, k2tog, psso) ten times, k5, yfwd, k1, yfwd, k5, k2togtbl.

Rnd 2: k.

Rep these 2 rows once more.

Change to yarn B and shape crown as folls, changing to dpns when necessary:

Rnd 1: k3tog, (k4, yfwd, k1, yfwd, k4, sl2, k3tog, p2sso) ten times, k4, yfwd, k1, yfwd, k4, k3togtbl. (*133 sts*).

Rnd 2(and every alt rnd): k.

Left: The beret is an extremely versatile piece of headwear, as it can be worn at many different angles on the head, depending on the look you want to achieve. A jaunty, asymmetric angle is the classic style, while worn pulled down over the forehead or looser at the back of the head are more modern trends.

Rnd 3: k2tog, (k4, yfwd, k1, yfwd, k4, sl1, k2tog, psso) ten times, k4, yfwd, k1, yfwd, k4, k2togtbl.
Rnd 5: k3tog, (k3, yfwd, k1, yfwd, k3, sl2, k3tog, p2sso) ten times, k3, yfwd, k1, yfwd, k3, k3togtbl. (*111 sts*).

Change to yarn A.
Rnd 7: k2tog, (k3, yfwd, k1, yfwd, k3, sl1, k2tog, psso) ten times, k3, yfwd, k1, yfwd, k3, k2togtbl.

After rnd 8, change to yarn B.
Rnd 9: k3tog, (k2, yfwd, k1, yfwd, k2, sl2, k3tog, p2sso) ten times, k2, yfwd, k1, yfwd, k2, k3togtbl. (*89 sts*).

After rnd 10, change to yarn A.
Rnd 11: k2tog, (k2, yfwd, k1, yfwd, k2, sl1, k2tog, psso) ten times, k2, yfwd, k1, yfwd, k2, k2togtbl.
Rnd 13: k3tog, (k1, yfwd, k1, yfwd, k1, sl2, k3tog, p2sso) ten times, (k1, yfwd) twice, k1, k3togtbl. (*67 sts*).

After rnd 14, change to yarn B.
Rnd 15: k2tog, (k1, yfwd, k1, yfwd, k1, sl1, k2tog, psso) ten times, (k1, yfwd) twice, k1, k2togtbl.
Rnd 17: k3tog, (yfwd, k1, yfwd, sl2, k3tog, psso) 10 times, yfwd, k1, yfwd, k3togtbl. *(45 sts)*.
Rnd 19: (k2tog) to last st, k1. (*23 sts*).
k1 rnd.

Break yarn, thread through rem 23 sts, pull up and secure. Fasten off yarn.

Block hat round a large dinner plate, spraying with a light mist of water, then set with steam and leaving to dry overnight.

Fair Isle Tank

Far right: The tank is a handy garment for layering in the inclement months of a seasonal calendar. The Fair Isle patterning will provide a seductive flash of colour under a solid jacket or cardigan or can be worn as the star piece over a shirt, turtleneck or tee.

During the early part of the twentieth century, Fair Isle knitwear became a popular trend, first appearing as golfing jumpers and the sleeveless "tank" for men. By the 1930s the vibrant multicoloured pattern had become more mainstream, fashionable for both sexes. In this pattern, all the traditional techniques of Fair Isle colourwork have been taken into account: the familiar "OXO" pattern, derived from the cross of the Scottish flag is there, but in addition there are abstract patterns inspired by the peaks, thistle flowers and other naturally occurring flora and fauna native to the Northern Isles of Scotland. Here, the vest plays with proportions of rib, therefore inserting larger areas of plain colour into the textured main. Added to the flattering rounded neck shaping, this leads to a contemporary, yet retro feel. Try wearing it with a rollneck for a modern yet classic look.

YARNS

2[2:3:3:3] x 25 g (1 oz) ball of Jamieson's Shetland Spindrift, 100% pure Shetland wool, 105 m (115 yds) in shade 107, mogit (yarn A)

1 x 25 g (1 oz) ball each of Jamieson's Shetland Spindrift 100% pure Shetland wool, 105 m (115 yds) in:
- yarn B: shade 390, daffodil
- yarn C: shade 764, cloud.
- yarn D: shade 660, lagoon.
- yarn E: shade 168, clyde blue.
- yarn F: shade 879, copper.
- yarn G: shade 147, moss.
- yarn H: shade 615, hyacinth.
- yarn I: shade 555, blossom.

Alternative yarns: any 4-ply yarn will substitute here. Perhaps experiment with qualities within this gauge to add texture to the patterning. Pure wools are generally great for Fair Isle work as the fibre will ensure the strands of yarn mesh together well and prevent gapping between the colours.

MEASUREMENTS

Bust

81–6	91–7	102–7	112–7	122–7 cm
32–34	36–38	40–42	44–46	48–50 in

Actual Size

92	102	112	120.5	130.5 cm
36	40	44	47½	51½ in

Length to Shoulder

45	46	48	51	53 cm
17¾	18	19	20	20¾ in

TENSION/GAUGE

32 sts and 32.5 rows to 10 cm (4 in) in Fair Isle pattern on 3.25 mm (US 3) knitting needles.

28 sts and 38 rows to 10 cm (4 in) in st st on 3.25 mm (US 3) knitting needles.

NOTIONS

Pair of 2.75 mm (US 2) knitting needles

Pair of 3.25 mm (US 3) knitting needles

Stitch holders

SPECIAL INSTRUCTIONS

ssp = slip, slip, purl – slip next 2 sts knitwise, place back onto the left needle and purl together.

Reading the Chart

Odd numbered rows are knit rows and the chart is read from right to left. Even numbered rows are purl rows and the chart is read from left to right.

There are a maximum of 2 colours to a row. Carry the colour not in use loosely on the WS so that the knitted fabric does not pucker.

Take all colours to the end of the row and twist the yarns together.

Chart shows full stitch repeat for each section of pattern, repeat these sts across whole row for each section. When 6 sections have been knit, go back and begin again from section 1.

Swap colours for second repeat of section, as desired.

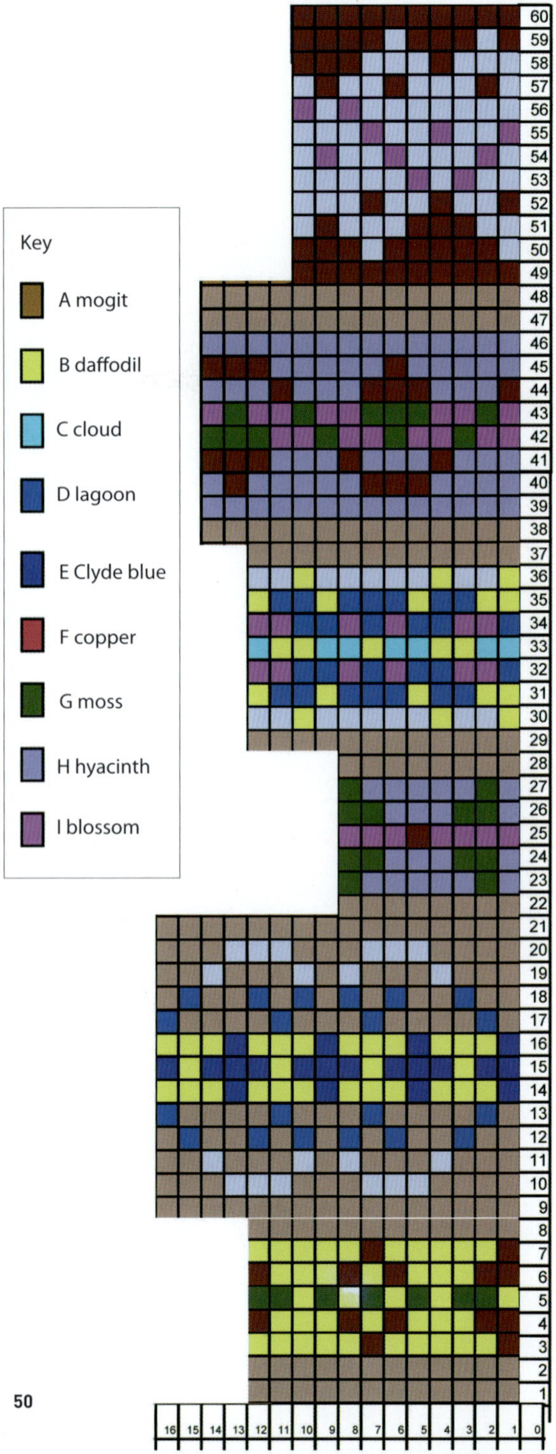

PATTERN

Back

Using 2.75 (US 2) knitting needles and yarn A, cast on 130[146:158:174:190] sts.

Row 1: (RS) [K2, p2] to last 2 sts, k2.

Row 2: (WS) P2, [k2, p2] to end.

Repeating rows 1 and 2 forms 2x2 rib. Cont in 2x2 rib until back measures 10[10:12:14:16] cm (4[4:4¾:5½:6¼] in), ending with a RSR.

Next row (increase row) (WS): P3 1[0:1:0:1] time, m1p 1[0:1:0:0] time, p6[4:6:0:4], m1p 1[1:1:0:0] times, [p7, m1p] 16[2:20:0:0] times, [p8, m1p] 0[13:0:21:21] times, [p7, m1p] 0[3:0:0:0] times, p6 [3:6:6:15], m1p 1[0:1:0:0] times, p3 1[0:1:0:0] time. 149[165:181:195:211] sts.

Change to 3.25 mm (US 3) knitting needles. Begin working from the chart working in st st.

Cont in Fair Isle pattern until back measures 22[22:23:26:28] cm (8½[8½:9:10¼:11] in) in from cast-on edge, ending with a WSR. **

Shape Armholes

Maintain continuity of the Fair Isle pattern throughout.

Cast off 6 sts at beg of next 2 rows. 137[153:169:183:199] sts.

Cast off 3 sts at beg of next 4 rows. 125[141:157:171:187] sts.

Cast off 2 sts at beg of next 10[12:14:15:17] rows. 105[117:129:141:153] sts.

Patt 0[0:0:1:1] row, ending with a WSR.

Next row (RS): K1, k2tog, patt to last 3 sts, ssk, k1. 103[115:127:139:151] sts.

Next row (WS): P1, ssp, patt to last 3 sts, p2tog, p1. 101[113:125:137:149] sts.

Rep last 2 rows 0[1:2:3:3] times and then the first of these 2 rows 0[1:1:0:0] time more. 101[107:115:125:137] sts.

Cont on these 101[107:115:125:137] sts without shaping until back measures 42[43:45:48:50] cm (16½[17:17¾:18¾:19½] in), ending with a WSR.

Shape Right Back Neck

Row 1 (RS): Patt 35[38:42:47:53] sts, turn and work on these sts only for right side of back neck. Leave rem 66[69:73:78:84] sts on a holder.

Row 2: Bind off 4 sts, patt to end. *31[34:38:43:49] sts.*

Row 3: Patt.

Row 4 and 5: Rep rows 2 and 3. *27[30:34:39:45] sts.*

Row 6: Bind off 3 sts, patt to end. 24[27:31:36:42] sts.

Row 7: Patt.

Row 8 and 9: Rep rows 6 and 7. *21[24:28:33:39] sts.*

Row 10: Bind off 2 sts, patt to end. *19[22:26:31:37] sts.*

If necessary, cont in patt without shaping until the right side of the back neck measures 45[46:48:51:53] cm (17¾[18¼:19:20:20¾] in, ending with a WSR.

If working to tension there should be approx 114[116:116:120:120] rows from the start of the Fair Isle pattern to the start of the shoulder shaping. If row 120 of the chart has been worked, start the chart again from row 1.

Shape Right Shoulder

Row 1 (RS): Bind off 9[11:13:15:18] sts, patt to end. *10[11:13:16:19] sts.*
Row 2: Patt.
Bind off rem sts.

Shape Left Back Neck

With RSF and maintaining continuity of Fair Isle pattern, rejoin yarns to 66[69:73:78:84] sts left on a holder for left back neck.
Row 1(RS): Patt centre 31 sts and leave on another holder, patt to end. *35[38:42:47:53] sts.*
Row 2(WS): Patt.
Row 3 (RS): Bind off 4 sts, patt to end. *31[34:38:43:49] sts.*
Row 4 and 5: Rep rows 2 and 3. *27[30:34:39:45] sts.*
Row 6: Patt.
Row 7: Bind off 3 sts, patt to end. *24[27:31:36:42] sts.*
Row 8 and 9: Rep rows 6 and 7. *21[24:28:33:39] sts.*
Row 10: Patt.
Row 11: Bind off 2 sts, patt to end. *19[22:26:31:37] sts.*

If necessary, cont in patt without shaping until left side of back neck measures 45[46:48:51:53] cm (17¾ [18¼:19:20:20¾] in), ending with a RSR.

If working to tension there should be approx 115[117:117:121:121] rows from the start of the Fair Isle pattern to the start of the shoulder shaping. If row 120 of the chart has been worked, start the chart again from row 1.

Shape Left Shoulder

Row 1 (WS): Bind off 9[11:13:15:18] sts, patt to end. *10[11:13:16:19] sts.*
Row 2: Patt.
Cast off rem sts.

Above: A low, rounded neckline on the tank somehow seems far more contemporary than a V-neck tank. It is just as versatile, but the organic shape is much prettier than the traditional version.

Front

Work as back to **. *149[165:181:195:211] sts.* Maintain continuity of pattern.

Shape Armhole and Left Front Neck

Row 1 (RS): Cast off 6 sts (1 st on RHN), patt 60[68:76:83:91] sts, turn and work on these 61[69:77:84:92] sts only for left side of front neck. Leave rem 82[90:98:105:113] sts on a holder.

*** Cast off 3 sts at armhole edge on 2 foll alt (RS) rows, cast off 2 sts at armhole edge on 5[6:7:7:8] foll alt (RS) rows, and then dec 1 st at armhole edge on next 2[5:7:9:9] rows while at the same time dec 1 st at neck edge, as explained below, on the next RSR then on foll 5 rows, dec 1 st at neck edge on 6 foll alt rows, dec 1 st on 6 foll 3rd rows, and then dec 1 st at neck edge on 6 foll 4th rows. *19[22:26:31:37] sts.*

Work dec at beg of RSRs as [k1, k2tog]. Work dec at end of RSRs as [ssk, k1]. Work dec at beg of WSRs as [p1, ssp]. Work dec at end of WSRs as [p2tog, p1].****

Cont in patt without shaping until left side of front neck measures 45[46:48:51:53] cm (17½[18:19:20:20¾] in), ending with a WSR.

If working to tension there should be approx 114[116:116:120:120] rows from the start of the Fair Isle pattern to the start of the shoulder shaping. If row 120 of the chart has been worked, start the chart again from row 1.

Shape Left Shoulder

Row 1 (RS): Bind off 9[11:13:15:18] sts, patt to end. *10[11:13:16:19].*
Row 2: Patt.
Bind off rem sts.

Shape Right Front Neck

With RSF and maintaining continuity of Fair Isle pattern, rejoin yarns to 82[90:98:105:113] sts left on a holder for right front neck.
Row 1 (RS): Patt centre 15 sts and leave on another holder, patt to end. *67[75:83:90:98] sts.*
Row 2: Cast off 6 sts, patt to end. *61[69:77:84:92] sts.*
Work as for left front neck from *** to **** reversing shapings.

Cont in patt without shaping until right side of front neck measures 45[46:48:51:53] cm (17½[18:19:20:20¾] in), ending with a RSR.

If working to tension there should be approximately 115[117:117:121:121] rows from the start of the Fair Isle pattern to the start of the shoulder shaping. If row 120 of the chart has been worked, start the chart again from row 1.

Shape Right Shoulder

Row 1 (WS): Bind off 9[11:13:15:18] sts, patt to end. *10[11:13:16:19] sts.*
Row 2: Patt.
Cast off rem sts.

Neckband

Block each piece. Join right shoulder seam using mattress stitch.
Using 2.75 mm (US 2) needles and yarn A, with RSF, pick up and k 59[63:67:71:75] sts down left front neck, k across 15 sts from holder at centre front neck while at the same time dec 3 sts evenly (12 sts), pick up and k59[63:67:71:75] sts up right front neck, pick up and k18 sts down right back neck, k across 31 sts from holder at centre back neck while at the same time dec 3 sts evenly (28 sts), and pick up and k18 sts up left back neck. 194[202:210:218:226] sts.

Starting with row 2, work 2 cm (¾ in) in 2x2 rib as for the back. Cast off in rib.

Armhole Bands (both alike)

Join left shoulder seam and left neckband seam using mattress stitch. Take 1 st into the seam for the neckband seam so that the 2x2 rib is uninterrupted.

Using 2.75 mm (US 2) needles and yarn A, with RSF, pick up and k59[61:63:65:67] sts from start of underarm bind off to shoulder seam of first half of armhole and then pick up and k59[61:63:65:67] sts from shoulder seam to end of underarm bind off for second half of armhole. *118[122:126:130:134] sts.*

Starting with row 2, work 2 cm (¾ in) in 2x2 rib as given for the back. Cast off in rib.

Make Up

Join side seams and the armbands at the underarm using mattress stitch, taking one whole stitch into the seam.

Far left: Fair Isle colourwork is an ancient technique with very traditional patterns. These can become bang up to date with the correct colourway – try bold and clashing colours for a striking tank or even shades of black, white and grey for a really avant-garde look.

The Thrifty Forties

Although a time of austerity and rationing, people in the 1940s were amazingly inventive with what they did have. Old garments would be remade into new pieces, decoration and trim added to worn collars or hems and knitting unravelled to be reused. Function, warmth and comfort were of prime importance, but because wool was used in the military effort, wool blends came into more common use. Fashion-wise, the decade was fairly bland with a limited colour palette of airforce blue, khaki and olive green and an angular silhouette of sharp shoulders and straight mid-calf skirts. The patterns in this chapter – for woollen stockings and a knitted turban, as well as the classic twinset and lace collar – show how the styles of the 1940s can still appear modern today, especially the strong shapes and wide shoulders.

Fashions and Patterns

With the Second World War in full swing at the beginning of the decade and rationing continuing into the latter half, the 1940s was a time of thrift when the "Make Do and Mend" ethos was born. Clothing was scarce in these hard times, so many people made their clothes from whatever materials they could find. Gentlemen's trousers, perhaps worn at the knee, could be made into skirts, holes in socks and knitwear were darned, and wedding dresses were made from recycled parachute silk.

A scarcity of wool meant that when children grew out of their jumpers or women got tired of particular pieces of knitwear, the items were unravelled and re-knitted into new garments, sometimes with various colours and types of yarn being worked into one piece. *Stitchcraft* was packed with tips on how to get the kinks out of yarn before re-knitting, or the best way to darn a hole. As one small wardrobe of clothes had to do for all occasions, most shirts and blouses had detachable collars so that you would only have to change the collar to brighten up an everyday outfit. There were also knitted versions of these collars, as well as fancy knitted bibs that could be worn over a plain shirt to give the appearance of an elaborate sweater.

The knitting pattern booklets of the day were filled with clothing that could be made and sent to soldiers fighting in Europe, such as balaclavas, gloves and socks with detachable heels and toes for ease of repair – just the worn-out sections could be re-knitted, thus saving wool. School children were often encouraged to knit for soldiers, attaching a label to the finished item with their name and a message for the lucky man who received a new pair of socks or a woolly hat.

Right: Influenced by the military styles of the Second World War, dresses, knitwear, suits and coats all had the pronounced angular shoulders so typical of 1940s fashion – here seen in the padded shoulders of this dress from 1947.

Left: In this colour advertisement from *Harper's Bazaar*, 1941, two models wear sports jersey skirt suits with matching hats, designed by S Katz & Co of Oxford Street, London. The wide-shouldered, narrow-waisted silhouette would prevail until Christian Dior launched his New Look in 1947.

Key themes

As fashion came to a near standstill during the war years, hand-knitting garments became one of the only ways in which women could express their individuality through their clothes. Highly patterned stitch techniques, such as moss stitch, twisted cables, lace and bobbles, were common and used to add prettiness to drab utilitarian outfits.

Women's fashions of the time were simple and practical. Twinsets were the main staple of most wardrobes, as they were associated with workwear and were worn for warmth, practicality and versatility. The cardigan was usually worn open, giving extra warmth to the short-sleeved, tight-fitting top. In general, clothes were more utilitarian than they had been in the 1930s, as many women were doing their part for the war effort in factories or fields rather than working at home. Shoulders were the focal point of sweaters, with hard, angular shapes as opposed to the soft, pretty silhouettes of the previous decade. Shorter sleeves, higher waists and fitted shapes were also common, as this type of styling used less yarn.

As the fashion focus shifted from Europe to New York and California, the American knitwear and sportswear industries thrived. Many home-grown knitting mills were able to produce fine cashmere and angora sweaters, particularly in demand by young women who wanted to emulate "Sweater Girls" such as Lana Turner, a beloved wartime pin-up. Designers Claire McCardell and Clare Potter boosted the fashion world with their all-American approach to casual fashion and emphasis on easy ready-to-wear pieces – hooded sweaters, long jersey shorts, swimwear and trouser suits.

In both the US and the UK, the government restricted not just materials but also colour dyes in an attempt to reduce the desire for new clothes and styles. Drab browns, greens and navy hid dirt and wear much better than lighter colours, and clothes made from these shades required less laundering. It wasn't until the war ended and Christian Dior heralded in his revolutionary New Look silhouette in 1947 that colour as well as volume returned to the fashion palette – with pale grey and blue being key Dior colours of the late 1940s.

The Thrifty Forties Mood Board

Knitting stitches rather than beading, taking the subdued wartime colour palette and brightening it up, and shaping the shoulder are all ideas used to translate the 1940s looks into the modernized patterns on the following pages.

Nylon
CHADWICK'S
WOOL and NYLON
Mending
428 MAROON
MADE IN ENGLAND
STITCHCRAFT
1941.
8D.
Bouton Lingerie

Twinset Sweater and Cardigan

A staple in most 1940s women's wardrobes, the twinset was extremely versatile and practical, a necessity in the years of rationing. There were many different variations of the style and stitch, with colour dependant on the yarn women managed to find or recycle. Most of the styles were short-waisted with a high neckline and sharp, ruched shoulders – from subtle, gathered versions through lightly padded knitted shoulderpads to huge, pointy affairs made from extra knitted pieces. This set has a more modestly shaped shoulder, which is both flattering and contemporary.

YARNS

13 [14:15] x 50 g (2 oz) balls of King Cole Merino DK, 100% pure new wool, 112 m (123 yds) in shade 708, lipstick red (yarn A).

3 [4:5] x 50 g (2 oz) balls of King Cole Merino DK, 100% pure new wool, 112 m (123 yds) in shade 787, fuschsia pink (yarn B).

Alternative yarns: Any DK weight yarn will do here. You can also knit this set in one colour if desired.

MEASUREMENTS

Cardigan

Bust

81–86	91–97	102–107 cm
32–34	36–38	40–42 in

Actual Size

89	100	110 cm
35	39¼	43¼ in

Length from Shoulder

56	59	60 cm
22	23¼	23½ in

Sleeve Seam

50	51	52 cm
19½	20	20½ in

Sweater

Bust

81–86	91–97	102–107 cm
32–34	36–38	40–42 in

Actual Size

86	97	107 cm
34	38	42 in

Length from Shoulder

51	54	57 cm
20	21¼	22½ in

Sleeve Seam

12	13	14 cm
4¾	5	5½ in

TENSION/GAUGE

24 sts and 28 rows to 10 cm (4 in) in st st using 3.75 mm (US 5) knitting needles.

27 sts and 30 rows to 10 cm (4 in) over rib pattern using 3.5 mm (US 4) knitting needles.

NOTIONS

Pair of 3.25 mm (US 3) knitting needles
Pair of 3.75 mm (US 5) knitting needles
Pair of 3.5 mm (US 4) knitting needles
6 x 1.5 cm (5/8 in) diameter buttons
Stitch holders
Darning needle

SPECIAL INSTRUCTIONS

Rib Pattern

Row 1(RS): p3[2:3], [k5, p2] to end.
Row 2: k2, [p5, k2], to end working k3[2:3] on last rep instead of k2.
Row 3: p3[2:3], *k2tog, yo, k1, yo, sl1, k1, psso, p2, rep from * to end.
Row 4: as row 2. Rep all rows for patt.

CARDIGAN PATTERN

Back

Using 3.25 mm (US 3) needles and yarn A, cast on 107[121:133] sts and work in rib as folls:
Row 1(RS): k2, [p1, k1] to last st, k1.
Row 2: p2, [k1, p1] to last st, p1.
Repeat last 2 rows for 12 cm (4¾ in) ending with a row 2, striping in 2 row stripes of yarn A and B.

Change to 3.75 mm (US 5) needles and yarn A, and work in st st, beg with a k row, until work measures 37[38:38] cm (14½[15:15] in) from cast-on edge, ending with a p row.

Shape Armholes

Cast off 8[10:11] sts at beg of next 2 rows, then dec 1 st at both ends of next 6[8:9] rows. *79[85:93] sts.*
Now dec 1 st at both ends of every foll alt row until 69[73:77] sts rem, ending with a p row.

Far left: The versatility of a twinset comes from the countless ways you can wear it, with the set worn together or singly. When worn together, the coloured yoke of the sweater is a bright focal point under the solid fabric of the cardigan.

Right: Choose vintage buttons for an authentic look; these are beautiful painted glass buttons that stand out well against the darker fabric and lend a casual feel to the set.

Work straight until work measures 19[21:22] cm (7½[8¼:8½] in) from beg of armhole shaping, ending with a WSR.

Shape Shoulders

Cast off 5[6:7] sts at beg of next 2 rows, then 5 sts at beg of foll 4 rows. Leave rem 39[41:43] sts on holder for back neck.

Left Front

Using 3.25 mm (US 3) needles and yarn A, cast on 64[70:76] sts and work in rib as folls:

Row 1(RS): k2, [p1, k1] to end.

Row 2: [p1, k1] to last 2 sts p2.

Repeat last 2 rows for 12 cm (4¾ in) ending with a row 2, striping in 2 row stripes alternately of yarn A and B.

Change to 3.75 mm (US 5) needles and yarn A, work in st st, beg with a k row, but leave last 10 sts of first k row on a holder/safety pin unworked.

Cont in st st on rem 54[60:66] sts until work measures 10[12:12] cm (4[4¾:4¾] in) from rib, ending with a p row. PM to indicate beg of neck.

Dec 1 st at neck edge of next row as folls:

Dec row: k to last 4 sts, k2tog, k2.

Dec as established at neck edge every foll 4th row 12 times, then every foll 6th row, until work measures 37[38:38] cm (14½[15:15] in) from cast-on edge, ending with a p row.

Shape Armholes

Cast off 8[10:11] sts at beg of next row, then dec 1 st at armhole edge on next 6[8:9] rows, then every foll alt row 5[6:8] times, while cont to dec for neck as established.

Work straight at armhole edge, while cont to dec for neck as established, until 15[16:17] sts rem. Work straight until front measures same as back to shoulder shaping, ending with a p row.

Cast off 5[6:7] sts at beg of next row and 5 sts at beg of foll 2 alt rows.

Right Front

Using 3.25 mm (US 3) needles and yarn A, cast on 64[70:76] sts and work in rib as folls:

Row 1(RS): [k1, p1] to last 2 sts, k2.

Row 2: p2, [k1, p1] to end.

Repeat last 2 rows for 12 cm (4¾ in) in alt 2-row stripes of yarn A and B, working a buttonhole at beg of 3rd row and then at 4 cm (1½ in) intervals as folls:

Buttonhole row (RS): rib 2, cast off 2, patt to end.

Next row: work in patt, casting on over the 2 buttonhole sts. End with a row 2, leaving last 10 sts on a holder unworked for buttonband.
Change to yarn A and 3.75 mm (US 5) needles and work as for left front, reversing all shapings.

Sleeves

Using 3.25 mm (US 3) needles and yarn A, cast on 51[57:63] sts and work in rib as folls:
Row 1(RS): k2, [p1, k1] to last st, k1.
Row 2: p2, [k1, p1] to last st, p1.
Repeat last 2 rows for 8 cm (3 in) ending with a row 2, striping in 2 row stripes alternately of yarn A and B.

Change to yarn A and 3.75 mm (US 5) needles and work in st st, beg with a k row, inc 1 st at either end of next and every foll 10th [9th:9th] row until there are 75[83:91] sts.

Cont straight until work measures 50[51:52] cm (19½[20:20½] in, ending with a p row.

Shape Cap

Cast off 8[10:11] sts at beg of next 2 rows, then dec 1 st at both ends of next 6[8:9] rows and every foll alt row until 35[35:37] sts.

Cont straight until cap measures 15[17:18] cm (6[6½:7] in) from beg of shaping. Cast off all sts.

Finishing

Join shoulder seams and then return to border ribbing on fronts. Using 3.25 mm (US 3) needles, keeping stripes correct, rib along sts from left front holder, work in rib a piece long enough to fit all along front edge to centre back. Cast off all sts.

On right front, rib along sts from right front holder, work in rib, making buttonholes as before at 4 cm (1½ in) intervals until 6 buttonholes are made, then cont straight in rib until the piece is long enough to fit all along front edge to centre back. Cast off all sts.

Sew down edgings neatly to fronts, then sew up centre back seam. Set in sleeves, gathering the fullness in neat pleats at the top of armhole (shoulder), using a small backstitch. Sew up side and underarm seams.

Sew on buttons.

Below left: The ribbed cuffs and edgings are slightly longer than 1940s sweaters to remain in proportion with the modern line, but they can be easily adjusted to bracelet-length, if desired.

Below right: The 1940s geometric shoulders are referenced here in the pretty, subtle ruching at the top of the sleeve. When setting in the cap, gather the fullness gently at the top of the armhole to achieve the shape.

SWEATER PATTERN

Back

Using 3.25 mm (US 3) needles and yarn A, cast on 91[105:117] sts and work in rib as folls:

Row 1(RS): k2, [p1, k1] to last st, k1.
Row 2: p2, [k1, p1] to last st, p1.
Repeat last 2 rows for 11 cm (4½ in) ending with a row 2.

Change to 3.75 mm (US 5) needles and work in st st, beg with a k row, inc 1 st at either end of 9th and every foll 10th row until 103[117:129] sts.

Work straight without increasing until work measures 33[34:35] cm (13[13¼:13¾] in) from cast-on edge, ending with a p row.

Shape Armholes

Cast off 8[10:11] sts at beg of next 2 rows, then dec 1 st at either end of next 5[6:7] rows. *77[85:93] sts.*

Now dec 1 st at either end of every foll alt row until 73[79:87] sts rem, ending with a p row.

Change to 3.5 mm (US 4) needles and yarn B and work in rib pattern for rem of back.

Work straight until piece measures 18[20:22] cm (7[7¾:8½] in) from beg of armhole shaping, ending with a WSR.

Shape Shoulders

Cast off 5 sts at beg of next 4 rows, then 5[6:7] at beg of foll 2 rows. *43[47:53] sts.*
Leave rem sts on holder for the back of the neck.

Front

Work as for the back until the armhole measures 13[15:17] cm (5[6:6½] in), ending with a WSR.
Next row: patt27[29:31], cast off 19[21:25], patt to end.

Work on these 27[29:31] sts for right front, dec 1 st at neck edge on every foll row until 15[16:17] sts rem. Work straight until front measures same as back to shoulder shaping, ending with a RSR.

Cast off 5 sts at beg of next and foll alt row then 5[6:7] sts at beg of foll alt row.

Rejoin yarn to left front neck and complete to match right, reversing all shapings.

Sleeves

Using 3.25 mm (US 3) needles and yarn A, cast on 57[65:73] sts and work in rib as folls:

Row 1(RS): k2, [p1, k1] to last st, k1.

Row 2: p2, [k1, p1] to last st, p1.

Repeat last 2 rows for 5 cm (2 in) ending with a row 2.

Change to 3.75 mm (US 5) needles and work in st st, beg with a k row, inc 1 st at either end of next and every foll 3rd[4th:4th] row until 67[75:83] sts. Work straight without increasing until work measures 12[13:14] cm (4¾[5:5½] in) from cast-on edge, ending with a p row.

Shape Cap

Cast off 8[10:11] sts at beg of next 2 rows, then dec 1 st at both ends of next 3 rows, then next 5[5:7] alt rows then every foll 4th row until 23[25:27] sts rem, ending with a p row.

Now dec 1 st at both ends of next 2 alt rows and every foll row until 9[11:13] sts rem. Cast off all sts.

Finishing

Sew up right shoulder seam.

With yarn A and 3.25 mm (US 3) needles, attach yarn to left front neck with RSF and pick up and knit 15 sts down left neck, 18[20:24] sts across centre neck, 15 sts up right neck and then 43[47:53] sts from holder at back neck. Work 4 rows 1x1 rib on these 91[97:107] sts. Cast off very loosely in rib.

Sew up rem shoulder seam, insert sleeves, then sew up side seams.

Far left: A lacy rib is utilized in the yoke to make a simple sweater more interesting without using up more yarn – a tip learned from the thrifty patterns of the 1940s.

Top left: The sweater is shaped at the waist to cling to the body in a flattering way, but is slightly longer than traditional patterns to suit a modern wearer.

Bottom left: The sweater is made with short sleeves in order to reduce bulkiness in the arm when worn with the cardigan.

Emerald Turban

The turban is a chic form of headwear, often associated with glamorous movie stars in their changing rooms inbetween takes. However, in the 1940s, the turban became a very quick and easy way to tie up the hair to keep it out of the way of heavy machinery while working. While the men went to war, the women took on all the traditionally masculine jobs, and there are many images of the time depicting women in overalls with handkerchiefs tied round their heads in cute bows. This version is a hybrid of the workaday kerchief and the elegant turban, creating a very simple yet modern take, which can be used to sweep back the hair, keep the head warm in winter or worn as a fashion statement.

Below: The hand-painted quality of this yarn gives a semi-solid colour, bestowing a beautiful texture onto a very simple stitch and pattern.

YARN

2 x 50 g (2 oz) balls of Louisa Harding Grace hand-dyed, 50% merino wool, 50% silk, 100 m (110 yds) in shade 7, olive green.

Alternative yarns: Any DK or sportweight yarn will be a good substitute here. You could try a solid or variegated yarn for different textures.

MEASUREMENTS

One size, to fit the average adult head, approximately 55 cm (21½ in).

To make the turban larger or smaller, simply knit the strip to a slightly longer or shorter length.

TENSION/GAUGE

42 sts and 30 rows to 10 cm (4 in) in 2x2 rib using 4 mm (US 6) knitting needles.

NOTIONS

Pair of 4 mm (US 6) knitting needles
Darning needle

PATTERN

Using 4 mm (US 6) needles, cast on 30 sts and work in 2x2 rib as folls:
Row 1: k2, *p2, k2 rep from * to end of row.
Row 2: p2, *k2, p2 rep from * to end of row.
Rep these 2 rows until work measures approx 105 cm (41¼ in).
Cast off all sts.

Making Up

Sew the 2 short ends of the strip together into a large loop. Twist the resulting loop once to create a figure of eight, then fold the figure-of-eight in half so that the loops overlap with the twist making the knot at the top of turban. Once you have a tidy arrangement, secure the shape at the twist with a few tacking stitches using the same yarn.

Left: The turban is worn with the knot at the top and slightly forward on the head. It makes a great alternative to a hat or ear muffs in cold weather or can be worn simply to keep the hair off the face.

Over-the-Knee Stockings

During the Second World War and the subsequent rationing, stockings were a luxury. Unable to get their hands on silk stockings, women stained their legs with tea and drew a seam down the back. As a result, woollen knitted versions could be seen in many knitting magazines, the height of economy in wartime. The pair here could be worn in many different ways – under a knee-length skirt, held up with suspenders, as ladies would have originally worn them; peeping over the top of wellies with shorts for a summer music festival; held up with a pretty ribbon threaded through the lace stitches; or just worn at home when the cold winter nights draw in.

YARN

5 x 50 g (2 oz) balls of Lang sock yarn 75% superwash new wool, 18% nylon, 7% acrylic, approximately 210 m (230 yd) plus 5 g (1/5 oz) reinforcement yarn, in shade 0122, tea.

Alternative yarns: any sockweight yarn. Try changing the fibre to silk or a more luxury fibre to create extravagant stockings.

TIP: This yarn has a handy reinforcement nylon thread to knit in at the heel and toe, a technique knitters performed in the war years to ensure their stockings lasted longer.

MEASUREMENTS

One size, to fit average UK sizes 4–6 (European 37–39, US sizes 6½–8½) adult feet, with instructions on where to elongate or shorten for different sizes of feet.

Width around calf (unstretched) is 24 cm (9½ in).
Width around thigh (unstretched) is 32.5 cm (12¾ in).

TENSION/GAUGE

36 sts and 40 rows to 10 cm (4 in) in st st using 2.75 mm (US 2) knitting needles.

NOTIONS

Pair of 2.75 mm (US 2) knitting needles
Set of 2.75 mm (US 2) double-pointed needles
Darning needle
Ribbon to tie at top if desired

SPECIAL INSTRUCTIONS

Lace Rib Pattern straight

Row 1: k3, *p3, k3, rep from * to end.
Row 2: p3, *k3, p3, rep from * to end.
Row 3: k3, *p3, k3 rep from * to end.
Row 4: p3, k3, *yrn p3tog, yon, k3, rep from * to last 3 sts, p3.
These 4 rows form pattern, rep for lace patt throughout.

Lace Rib Pattern in round

Rnd 1–3: k3, *p3, k3, rep from * to end.
Rnd 4: k3, p3,*yon, k3tog, yrn, p3, rep from * to last 3 sts, k3.
These 4 rows form the pattern, rep for lace patt throughout.

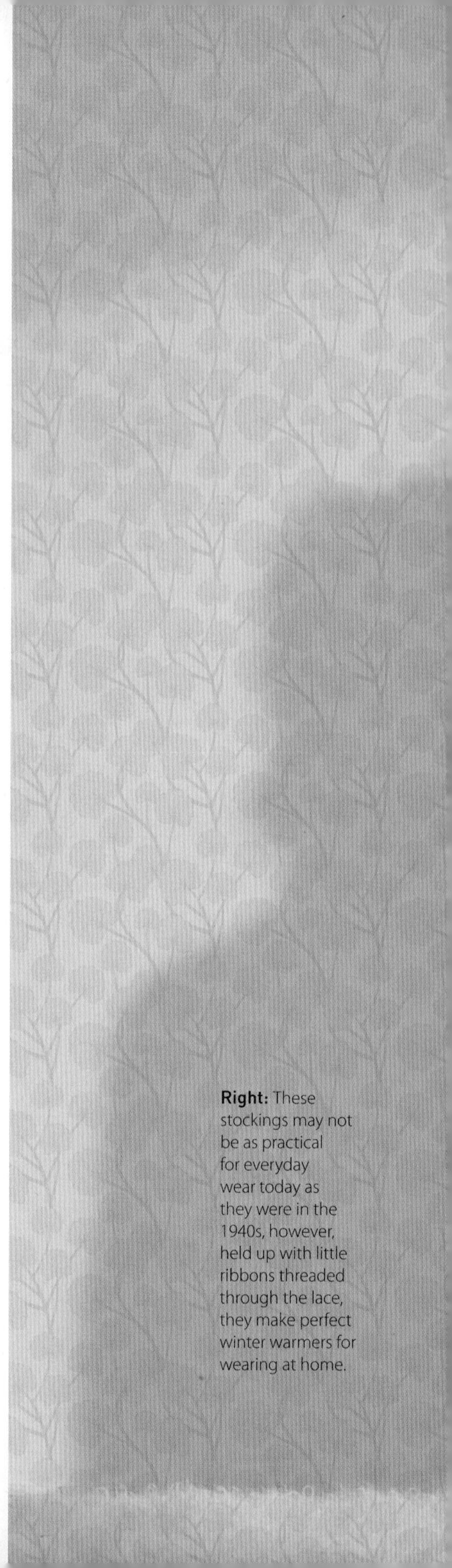

Right: These stockings may not be as practical for everyday wear today as they were in the 1940s, however, held up with little ribbons threaded through the lace, they make perfect winter warmers for wearing at home.

Right: Cables and twisted ribs were a great way of prettifying plain knits in the 1940s and here they have the added bonus of making the resulting fabric even warmer.

Right: The shaping of the leg at the calf, knee and thigh are all worked into a stocking stitch seam to create a pretty feature.

PATTERN

Using 2.75 mm (US 2) needles, cast on 117 sts.

Row 1(RS): k3, *p3, k3, rep from * to end.

Row 2: p3, *k3, p3, rep from * to end.

Rep last 2 rows until work measures 5 cm (2 in), ending with a row 2.

Beg straight lace patt and work straight until piece measures approx 32 cm (12 ½ in), ending with a row 2.

Decrease for leg as folls:

Row 1: k3, k3tog, patt to last 6 sts, sl 2, k1, p2sso, k3. *113 sts.*

Cont in pattern as established, working odd decreased sts at beg/end of row into st st as suitable, decreasing 4 sts on every following 8th row as on row 1, until 85 sts rem, then on every following 6th row until there are 69 sts.

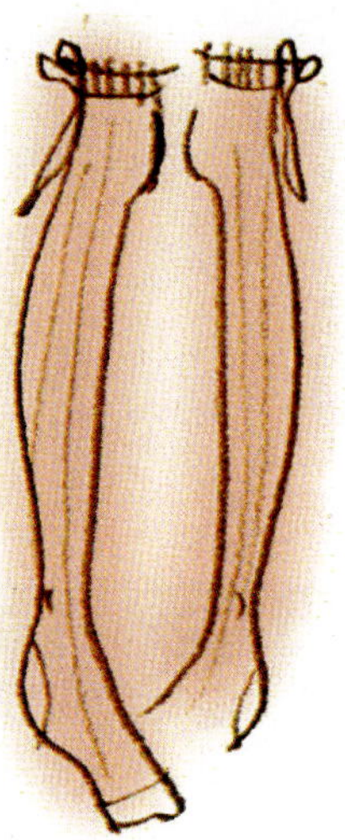

Cont straight in patt until work measures 58 cm (23 in) ending with RSF.

Divide sts for heel as folls, changing to dpns:

k15 on a dpn, patt over next 39 sts on separate dpn, and leave for instep, k14, inc1 into next st on another dpn, then k15 first sts again. These 31 sts form the heel.

Work back and forth on these 31 heel sts in st st, slipping the first st of every row.

Turn heel, working with the working yarn and 1 strand of accompanying reinforcement thread, held together:

Row 1: k21, sl1, k1, psso, turn.

Row 2: p12, p2tog, turn.

Row 3: k12, sl1, k1, psso, turn.

Rep rows 2 and 3 until all sts are worked (break off reinforcement thread).

Next row: k7, thus completing heel (6 unworked sts on heel).

Cont in the rnd as folls:

Using spare needle (1 st dpn), k6 heel sts, pick up and k16 sts along side of heel, using 2nd dpn, patt across 39 instep sts (now using lace rib patt in rnd) using 3rd needle, pick up and knit 16 sts along rem side of heel, k7 heel sts. *84 sts.*

Shape Instep

Rnd 1: k to instep, patt across instep, k to end of rnd.

Rnd 2: dpn1: k to last 3 sts, k2tog, k1, dpn2: pattern across, dpn 3: k1, sl1, k1, psso, k to end.

Rep these 2 rnds until 70 sts rem.

Cont on these 70 sts in the rnd without shaping until the work measures 14 cm (5½ in) from where sts were knitted up at the heel, or until desired length of foot, minus 5 cm (2 in), is reached.

Next rnd: 1st needle: k, 2nd needle: k1, sl2, k1, p2sso, k to last 4 sts, k3tog, k1, 3rd needle: k. *66 sts.*

Rep last rnd once more. *62 sts.*

Shape Toe

With the working yarn and 1 strand of accompanying reinforcement thread, held together, work as folls:

Rnd 1: 1st needle: k to last 3 sts, k2tog, k1, 2nd needle: k1, sl1, k1, psso, k to last 3 sts, k2tog, k1, 3rd needle: k1, sl1, k1, psso, k to end,

Rnds 2 and 3: k.

Rep these 3 rnds until 38 sts rem, graft rem sts or cast off using 3 needles.

Lacy Collar

This pretty pattern derives from the days when collars and cuffs were often separate from garments, both for ease of laundering and for allowing easy transformation of a simple blouse, dress or knit from casual daywear to "Sunday Best". Here, the lacy collar can be used to add interest to a plain jumper or be worn alone as a beautiful, delicate necklace or neckpiece.

YARN

1 x 50 g (2 oz) ball of Blue Sky Alpaca Silk, 50% alpaca, 50% silk, 133 m (146 yds) in shade 133, blush

Alternative yarns: any yarn will do, as tension is not essential, however, the collar will be more delicate in lace, 4-ply or sportweight yarns. Try a variety of fibres for differing effects, or yarns that are pre-beaded to make the piece more glamorous.

Left: A removable collar was often used in the war period to transform a functional jumper into a decorative piece for church-going or eveningwear. Pair this version with a round-neck jumper as here, or for a contemporary twist wear it as a necklace with a low-necked dress.

Below: A delicate vintage button makes a practical yet beautiful solution to secure the collar – try wearing it at the front neck to show it off! Alternatively, the collar can be worn with the button at the back or even at the side.

MEASUREMENTS

Collar measures approximately 42 cm (16 ½ in) around the neck.

TENSION/GAUGE

Tension is not essential.

NOTIONS

Pair of 3.5 mm (US 4) knitting needles
1 button, approx 1 cm (½ in) in diameter

PATTERN

Using 3.5 mm (US 4) knitting needles, cast on 81 sts.

k1, * cast off next 4sts, (1st rem on RHN), rep from * to end of row. *17 sts.*

*k1, yfwd, rep from * to end, k1. *33 sts.*
Work 4 rows st st, beg with a k row.

k1, *yfwd, sl1, k2tog, psso, rep from * to last 2sts, yfwd, k2tog. *23 sts.*
Next row: p.
Next row: k.
Next row: p.
k2* yfwd, sl1, k2tog, psso, rep from * to end. *16 sts.*
Next row: p.
Next row: k.
Next row: p.
k1, *yfwd, sl1, k2tog, psso, rep from * to end. *11 sts.*
Next row: p.
Next row: k.
Next row: p.
(k2tog) to last st, k1. *6 sts.*
Do not cast off, break yarn. Leave these sts on a holder.

Make 4 more scallops in the same way.

To join together, use 3.5 mm (US 4) needles, with RSF. Pick up 8 sts along the flat edge to the right of the sts on the first scallop, knit along 6 sts from holder as folls:
(k2tog) to end.

Pick up 8 sts from opposite flat edge. With the same needles and yarn, rep this process along each of the rem 4 scallops, joining them together. Cast on 5 sts at the end of this row. *100 sts.*

Cont on these 100 sts for a foll 3 rows garter st, next row, k to last 3 sts, yfwd, k2tog, k1. Buttonhole made.

Work 2 more rows garter st.
Cast off all sts.

Weave in all ends and attach button to the opposite end of collar to that of the buttonhole.

The Fabulous Fifties

With the Second World War over, the 1950s embraced an optimism and enthusiasm that had lain dormant for years. Colour, shape and liveliness of design were back in fashion, and the hourglass silhouette lent a decorative, feminine and rather frivolous tone. Handknitting was revitalized by new synthetic fibres, which made easy-to-launder clothes that kept their shape, and garments were fully fashioned – that is, knitted to shape and not cut and sewn. A plethora of collar, sleeve and dress styles led to a boom in knitting patterns of every shape and sort. In this chapter key trends, such as the cowl, dolman sleeve, full-skirted dress and embroidered cardigan, are updated for today.

Knitting and Fashion

In a strong reaction to the frugalities of war, Dior launched his "New Look" silhouette in 1947, with its full skirt, feminine, cinched-in waist and softly rounded shoulders. This was to become the iconic look of the 1950s, celebrating the end of clothes' coupons and fabric rationing. Suddenly clothing featured large dolman sleeves, oversized collars and a surplus of cloth… and women loved it. From housewife to teenager, this was the silhouette adopted by all.

Mass production in the ready-to-wear market also became big business, making fashion more affordable to everyone. Although in the absence of a homogenized high street, this had little effect on the popularity of hand-knitting and -sewing, both which remained key ways to recreate trends from Paris.

Yarns began to incorporate more manmade fibres, and chunkier weights became more common. Angora was a popular choice for the "Sweater Girl" style of fitted jumpers, while cashmere was the luxury choice to covet, especially made up into delicate pastel-coloured twinsets, or "sweater sets". Patterns began to be written with different size options and incorporated all sorts of techniques and a huge variety of colours. The baby boom also heralded a boom in knitting for babies, young children and family groups.

Left: The New Look silhouette is perfectly represented here in the nipped-in waist and full skirt of this two-piece slate blue dress by Heatherlane from 1955.

Key themes

The 1950s are often referenced in today's fashions, and trends from the time can still look modern when styled correctly – the overall effect being feminine, sensual and acknowledging women's natural curves. A recurring theme found in knitting patterns from the era is the tight, fitted sweater, worn with pointed bras to give the familiar "Sweater Girl" silhouette, which was especially effective when teamed with very full or very tight pencil skirts. Another style was the chunkier, looser-fitting jumper worn over close-fitting tailored trousers with pumps, which gave a "Beatnik" look.

By the late 1950s, the knitted sweater dress was a mainstream choice. Often seen with crew or cowl necks and made from acrylic or lambswool yarns, the dresses were figure-hugging, long and lean. Cardigans became more decorative with elaborate beading, novelty buttons and sequins, typified by such knitwear designers as Helen Bond Carruthers and Bonnie Cashin, and were worn over both day dresses and eveningwear. Sleeves were often bracelet or three-quarter length to show off shapely wrists, and typical collar styles were boatneck, U-shape, shawl, square-neck and Peter Pan.

Right: The dolman sleeve was a decade classic. Here a 1955 advertisement promotes a Forstmann wool ensemble. Forstmann was originally a yarn manufacturer.

The Fabulous Fifties Mood Board

The pretty pastel colours of the 1950s are so sugar-coated and sweet that they are irresistible to use in knitted projects, and soft yarns such as angora and cashmere perfectly emphasize the decade's obsession with femininity, luxury and ladylike elegance. To tap into the decade's trend for decoration, look for retro novelty buttons, beads, sequins, satin ribbon trim and bows with which to embellish your knitting.

CLARK'S
FINE
FILOSHEEN
GRIST
MENDING
4 ENDS
ALL KINDS OF HOSIERY ETC
20 YARDS
F541
PALE SALMON PINK
18 METRES
No40

Left and above: The cowl can be worn in several ways – around the head for added warmth, as left, looped once around the neck to hang low to the front or double-wrapped around the neck, as above.

Cosy Ice-Cream Cowl

Pastels were the popular colours of the decade – soft ice-cream shades were seen in everything from fridges to cars – so it is no surprise that they filtered into fashion. Signature colours were pale pink, pale blue, maize, amethyst, lilac, seafoam green and kingfisher blue; clean, soft, innocent and decidedly feminine, the palette was found its way into twinsets, prom dresses and full-circle skirts. This cowl takes inspiration from the pastel shades of the time, with a hint of strong green in a stripe to give it a modern edge, and is extremely practical and very quick to knit, especially using modern circular needles to work the loop in the round, which means no sewing up!

YARNS

2 x 50 g (2 oz) balls each of Blue Sky Alpacas sportweight, 100% baby alpaca, 100 m (110 yds) in shade 514, pale aqua (yarn A) and shade 500, natural white (yarn B).

1x 50 g (2 oz) ball each of Blue Sky Alpacas sportweight, 100% baby alpaca, 100 m (110 yds) in shade 520, avocado (yarn C) and 516, petal pink (yarn D).

Alternative yarns: any sportweight or DK yarn will fit in with this pattern, but as it is a simple shape you could vary the weight of the yarn to achieve a different size of cowl.

MEASUREMENTS

One size. Approximately 99 cm (39 in) circumference and 31 cm (12¼ in) deep.

TENSION/GAUGE

18 sts to 10 cm (4 in) in moss (seed) st using 3.5 mm (US 4) circular knitting needles.

NOTIONS

3.5 mm (US 4), 80 cm (30 in) long circular knitting needles
Darning needle

SPECIAL INSTRUCTIONS

Moss (seed) st worked in the round
Rnd 1: (p1, k1) to end of rnd.
Rnd 2: (k1, p1) to end of rnd.

Stripe Pattern
6 of yarn A
8 of yarn D
2 of yarn C
4 of yarn B
2 of yarn C
8 of yarn A
6 of yarn B
4 of yarn D
6 of yarn A
8 of yarn B
6 of yarn A
8 of yarn B
4 of yarn C
2 of yarn A
2 of yarn C
8 of yarn D
6 of yarn B
6 of yarn D
2 of yarn B
Rep for pattern.

Above: The moss, or seed, stitch is a very basic technique yet presents one of the prettiest knitted fabrics. It is perfect for a simple 1950s project like this cosy cowl.

PATTERN

Using 3.5 mm (US 4) circs, cast on 178 sts and join for working in the round, PM at beg of rnd. Work in moss st in stripe pattern, as left, until work measures 31 cm (12¼ in).

Cast off all sts very loosely in pattern, weave in all ends and block lightly to shape.

Lacy "New Look" Dress

After the "Make Do and Mend" ethos of the previous decade, the 1950s celebrated the end of clothes rationing with the New Look, straight from Paris, which saw full skirts made in plentiful yards of fabric. This chic lace dress takes the scoop neck and full-skirt of that classic Christian Dior silhouette and creates an incredibly feminine dress suitable for any decade, past, present or future. The dress is worked in the round to give a seamless finish, with the skirt worked bottom up and the bodice top down to utilize the scalloped edge of the lace pattern.

YARN

3[3:4] x 50 g (2 oz) balls of Malabrigo Lace, 100% baby merino, 430 m (470 yds) in shade 62, marine.

Alternative yarns: Any lace-weight yarn will substitute; a lightweight yarn is probably preferable with this much fabric, however, a silk mix could be a great summer alternative that gives added sheen.

NOTE: This pattern uses negative ease to achieve a close fit – it will stretch to fit the curves of your body through the give in the lace stitch.

MEASUREMENTS

Bust

XS	S	M	L
76–81	81–86	91–97	102–107 cm
30–32	32–34	36–38	40–42 in

Actual Size

72	88	96	104 cm
28½	34½	37	41 in

Actual Hip

104	104	112	128 cm
41	41	44	50½ in

Bodice Length

37	38	40	41 cm
14½	15	15¾	16¼ in

Skirt Length

58	58	60	62 cm
22¾	22¾	23½	24¼ in

TENSION/GAUGE

25 sts and 32 rows to 10 cm (4 in) in st st using 4.5 mm (US 7) knitting needles.

NOTE: Blocked measurements will be significantly different to unblocked. When measuring length over the garment, take into consideration that the fabric will be significantly longer when blocked.

NOTIONS

Pair of 4.5 mm (US 7) knitting needles
60 cm (24 in) long circulars with tips suitable for lace knitting
80 cm (32 in) long circulars with tips suitable for lace knitting
Set of 3.75 mm (US 5) double-pointed needles
Stitch markers in different colours
Stitch holders
Darning needle

SPECIAL INSTRUCTIONS

Entire dress is knitted in the round, from the bottom up for the skirt and from the top down for the bodice. The pieces are then seamlessly grafted together at the waist ribbing.

Lace Pattern (in round)

Rnd 1: [yo, k3, sl1, k2tog, psso, k3, yo, k1] to end.
Rnd 2: k.
Rnd 3: k1 [yo, k2, sl1, k2tog, psso, k2, yo, k3] to end, ending last rep k2 instead of k3.
Rnd 4: k.
Rnd 5: yo, k2tog, yo, k1, sl1, k2tog, psso, k1, yo, k1, yo, sl1, k2tog psso, *yo, k1, yo, k1, sl1, k2tog, psso, k1, yo, k1, yo, sl1, k2tog psso, rep from * to end, ending last rep with sl1, k1, psso.
Rnd 6: k.

Right: A "New Look" style of dress never goes out of fashion and is especially useful for parties and weddings. Wear this one with a layered tulle petticoat underneath to make the most of the full lace skirt. Choosing a complementary-coloured petticoat underneath will add a whole different dimension to the knitting as the colour will show through the lace holes.

Right: The dress is worked in two halves – the bodice and the skirt – and then seamed at the waist in order to make the most of the scallops along the cast-on edge of the lace pattern.

PATTERN

Skirt

Using 4.5 mm (US 7) needles, cast on 460[460:480:520] sts, join for working in round, PM at beg of rnd.

Work 2 rnds in garter st.

Work one whole pattern repeat, but instead of working yo increase, work an m1 increase for every yo, then cont normally in patt as stated for 3 full pattern repeats, PMs on last rnd of different colour to end of rnd marker as folls:

Next rnd: patt 60[60:60:70] sts, PM, patt 110[110:120:120], PM, patt 120[120:120:140], PM, patt 110[110:120:120], PM, patt to end of rnd.

Cont in patt, dec on every 3rd row as folls, keeping lace pattern as correct as possible until 260 [260:280:320] sts rem.

**Dec rnd (ignore end of rnd marker in decs): ***patt to 2 sts before marker, sl1, k1, psso, sl marker, k2tog; rep from * 3 further times, patt to end.

Work straight in patt until work measures 58[58:60:62] cm (22¾ [22¾:23½:24¼] in) or desired length to waist, ending with last rnd of patt.

Next rnd: dec 80[40:40:60] sts evenly across rnd. *180[220:240:260] sts.*

Change to 3.75 mm (US 5) dpns and work in 1x1 rib for 6 cm (2¼ in). Leave all sts on holder for the waist.

Bodice

Using smaller 4.5 mm (US 7) needles cast on 180[220:240:260] sts and join for working in round, PM at beg of rnd.

Work 2 rnds in garter st.

Work one whole patt repeat, but instead of working yo increase, work an m1 increase for every yo, then cont normally in patt as stated for 1 full patt repeat, PMs on last rnd of different colour to end of rnd marker as folls:

Next rnd: patt 40[50:50:60] sts, PM, patt 10[10:20:20], PM, patt 80[100:100:100], PM, patt 10[10:20:20], PM, patt to end of rnd.

Cont in patt, inc on every even (knit) row as folls, knitting all new sts instead of working into pattern until there are 220[260:280:300] sts.

Inc rnd (ignore end of rnd marker in decs): *patt to 1 st before marker, inc 1, sl marker, inc 1; rep from * 3 times more.

Cont straight in pattern – knitting over all increased sts until 4[4:5:5] repeats have been worked from beg of increases, ending with row 5 of final repeat.

Shape Armholes

Next rnd: k35[45:45:55], place 40[40:50:50] sts on holder for sleeve, k70[90:90:90], place 40[40:50:50] sts on second holder for sleeve, k to end of rnd.

Next rnd: patt across 35[45:45:55] sts, cast on 20[20:30:30] sts for armhole, patt across 70[90:90:90] sts, cast on 20[20:30:30] sts for armhole, patt to end of rnd.

Work straight in patt until bodice measures approx 27[28:29:30] cm (10½[11:11½:12] in) from armhole, or desired length from armhole, ending with a row 6.

Leave all sts on holder.

Block both pieces in sections and leave to dry before moving on to the next section. For example, work skirt in panels of 4 or 6 and bodice; block front then back.

Joining

Graft body sts to skirt ribbing sts, placing start of rnd of skirt to one side of body – under an armhole.

Using 3.75 mm (US 5) dpns, rejoin yarn to underarm with RSF and pick up and k 30[30:40:40] sts from underarm and work in 1x1 rib from 40[40:50:50] sts on holder.

Join for working in the rnd, PM at beg of rnd, and work 3 foll rows in 1x1 rib. Cast off very loosely in rib.
Rep for rem armhole.

Left: Ribbing is used to ensure the dress pulls in at that essential part of a 1950s silhouette – the waspish waist – yet is still easy to pull on over the head and shoulders.

Right: A casual jumper in the 1950s style is still eminently wearable today with jeans or Capri pants and some flat ballet pumps. It could even be worn over a long-line pencil skirt for a preppy look.

Dolman Sleeve Sweater

It is rare to see bulky yarns used in vintage knitting patterns, however some did occur and this pattern takes inspiration from those to create a simple, quick-to-knit sweater. The sweater is knit in the round for the body then, working the front and back straight, the dolman sleeves are knit in the same piece as the body, grafted at the shoulders for a seamless-looking jumper. The dolman sleeve, popular during the late 1930s and early 1940s in elegant eveningwear, disappeared during the war years due to the extra fabric required, but it made a comeback in the 1950s as part of the feminine New Look. Wear the cuffs long or, for a more authentic period look, fold them back to bracelet length.

YARN
10[11:12] x 50g (2 oz) balls GGH Aspen, 50% fine merino wool, 50% acrylic, 58 m (63 yds) in shade 60, mustard.

Alternative yarns: any bulky-weight yarn will do here. The yarn used in this pattern is mixed with a manmade fibre, which makes it very light and ensures that the yarn keeps its shape and does not stretch too much. It may be worth bearing this in mind when choosing a substitute.

MEASUREMENTS

Bust

81–86	91–97	102–107 cm
32–34	36–38	40–42 in

Actual Size

92.5	101.5	110.5 cm
36½	40	43½ in

Length from Shoulder

53	56	59 cm
20¾	22	23¼ in

Sleeve Seam

47	49	51 cm
18½	19¼	20 in

TENSION/GAUGE
11 sts and 16 rows to 10 cm (4 in) in st st using 8 mm (US 11) knitting needles.

NOTIONS
7 mm and 8 mm (US 11), 60 or 80 cm (24 or 32 in) long, circular needles
7 mm (US 11), 40 cm (16 in) long, circular needles or double-pointed needles
Stitch holders
Darning needle

PATTERN
Using the smaller needles, cast on 102[112:122] sts and join for working in the round, PM for beg of rnd. Work 6 cm (2¼ in) in 1x1 rib.

Change to the larger needles and st st until work measures 26[28:30] cm (10¼[11:11¾] in) from cast-on edge.

Back
Next row: k51[56:61], leave rem sts on holder for front.

Shape Sleeves
Cont in st st, cast on 8[8:9] sts at beg of next 8[4:8] rows, then 9 sts at beg of foll 2[6:2] rows. *133[142:151] sts.*

Work 12[13:14] cm (4¾[5:5½] in) straight in st st on these sts, ending with a p row.

*k to last 8[8:9] sts, turn leaving these sts unworked and work back to last 8[8:9] sts, turn, rep from *4[0:3] times more, then k to last 9[9:10] sts, turn leaving these sts unworked and work back to last 9[9:10] sts, turn, rep from *1[5:2] times more, leave centre 17[18:19] sts on holder for back neck, and each 58[62:66] sts for sleeves on separate holders.

Right: Dolman sleeves and chunky yarn were popular decade details that remain fabulous choices today for a quick and fuss-free knit.

Right: The satisfying, chunky ribbed collar can be worn standing up to provide extra warmth or folded over for an open-collar style.

Far right: The cuffs are also versatile; wear them folded back to create elegant bracelet-length sleeves and show off a beautiful piece of vintage jewellery.

Front

Rejoin yarn to k51[56:61] sts for front.

Work as for back until armhole measures 8[9:10] cm (3¼[3½:4] in), ending with a p row.

Shape Neck and Sleeves

While continuing to work in patt to shape sleeves, work neck as folls:
Next row: k66[71:75], turn and leave rem sts unworked.

Work on left sleeve and neck as folls: Cont shaping sleeve as set for back, while dec 1 st at beg of next and every foll 3rd row on neck edge until 8[9:9] decreases have been made in all at neck edge. Cont straight at neck edge while shaping rem of sleeve.

Rejoin yarn to opposite side, at neck edge with RSF, leaving first st on safety pin for small and large sizes only.

Work as folls on these k66[71:75] sts.
Next row: k2tog, k to end.

Cont shaping sleeve as set for back, while dec 1 st at beg of every foll 3rd row on neck edge until 8[9:9] decreases have been made in all at neck edge. Cont straight at neck edge while shaping rem of sleeve.

Graft right shoulder and sleeve sts together, then left shoulder and sleeve sts.

Collar

Using the smaller circs or dpns, join yarn to right neck, pick up and k25 sts up right neck, k across 17[18:19] sts on holder for back neck, then pick up and k25 sts down left neck and work 1[0:1] centre front neck st.

Join for working in the rnd and work on these 68[68:70] sts for approx 8 cm (3 in):

Next row: rib 52[52:54] sts, turn, leaving rem sts unworked.
Next row: rib 36[36:38] sts, turn, leaving rem sts unworked.
Next row: rib 44[44:46] sts, turn, leaving rem sts unworked.
Next row: rib 52[52:54] sts, turn, leaving rem sts unworked.
Next row: rib 60[60:62] sts, turn, leaving rem sts unworked
Next row: rib across row.
Cast off all sts loosely in rib.

Sew up small seam at centre front of neck, fold over neck and secure at the front neck to prevent the collar from flipping.

Cuffs

With RSF and smaller circular needles or a pair of dpns, rejoin yarn to edge of sleeve at cuff. Pick up and k43[45:47] sts along cuff and work 10 cm (4 in) in 1x1 rib.
Rep for rem cuff.

Make Up

Join underarm and cuff seams.

Lilac Beaded Cardigan

Twinsets continued to be a wardrobe staple in the 1950s, yet in addition to being a practical item in the wardrobe, they began to be made in elegant and embellished forms in new colours and styles. No longer part of the staple, working wardrobe, cardigans were made with luxury fibres such as the fluffy angora, which is incredibly warm and soft, but also looks ultra feminine. As many dresses were sleeveless, the pretty cardigan was a glamorous cover-up and casual alternative to the jacket. Often highly embellished with beads or sequins, they were cropped short at the wrist to display a pretty bracelet and at the waist to show off the nipped-in hourglass figure.

Authentic 1950s cardigans and twinsets are some of the most sought-after vintage items today, particularly those embellished with sequins, trapunto, beadwork, lace or appliqué. This pattern is knitted on circular needles, working the piece all at once to give a virtually seamless sweater.

Far left: This "light as a feather" cardigan is a breeze to make and so easy to wear. Pair it with a shift dress for evening or throw it over a T-shirt and jeans for a warm and chic-yet-casual outfit.

YARN

4 [5:6] x 50 g (2 oz) balls Orkney Angora St Magnus 50/50 DK, angora and lambswool, 200 m (218 yds) in shade 15, lavender.

Alternative yarns: Any lightweight DK or sportweight yarns. This yarn is incredibly light and warm, due to the fluffy angora, which makes it a dream to wear, but also goes a long way due to its yardage. Take this into account when substituting.

MEASUREMENTS

Bust

81–86	91–97	102–107 cm
32–34	36–38	40–42 in

Actual Size

92	102	112 cm
36¼	40	44 in

Length

47.5	51	53 cm
18¾	20	20¾ in

Sleeve Seam

35	36	37 cm
13¾	14	14½ in

TENSION/GAUGE

24 sts and 30 rows to 10 cm (4 in) in st st using 3.75 mm (US 5) knitting needles.

NOTIONS

3 mm (US 2.5), 60–80 cm (24–32 in) long circular needles
3.75 mm (US 5), 60–80 cm (24–32 in) long circular needles
Set of 3 mm (US 2.5) double-pointed needles
Set of 3.75 mm (US 5) double-pointed needles
Stitch holders
Stitch markers
Darning needle
8 x 1 cm (½ in) diameter buttons
Beads (optional)

Right: The fully-fashioned raglan sleeves and yoke worked in the round make a feature of the construction and create a near-seamless garment with beautiful finishing.

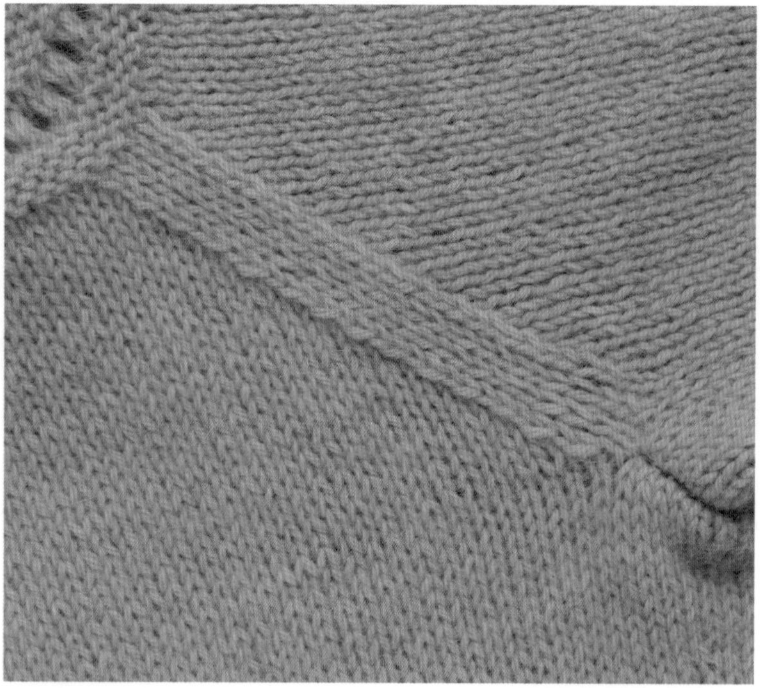

PATTERN

Sleeves (make 2)

Using 3 mm (US 2.5) dpns, cast on 53[59:65] sts and join for working in the rnd, PM at beg of rnd.

Work in 1x1 rib as folls:
Rnd 1: k1, *p1, k1; rep from * to end of rnd. Row 1 forms patt, rep for approx 6 cm (2½ in).

Change to 3.75 mm (US 5) dpns and st st. Inc 1 st at either end of every 5th rnd, until 81[89:97] sts.

Work straight on these sts until work measures 35[36:37] cm (13¾[14:14½] in).

Cast off 6[7:8] sts at beg of next rnd.

Turn and cont working straight, casting off 6[7:8] sts at beg of next row. Leave these 69[75:81] sts on a holder.

Body

Using 3 mm (US 2.5) circs, cast on 173[197:221] sts and work in 1x1 rib as folls:
Row 1: k2, *p1, k1; rep from * to last st, k1.
Row 2: p2, *k1, p1; rep from * to last st, p1. Rows 1 and 2 form rib pattern, rep until rib measures 3 cm (1¼ in), ending with a row 2.

Change to 3.75 mm (US 5) circs and st st, beg with a k row. Work 6 rows.
Row 7: k42[48:54], m1, PM, k2, PM, m1, k85[97:109], m1, PM, k2, PM, m1, k to end. *177[201:225] sts.*

Work 3 rows st st beg with p row.
Inc row: [k to marker, m1, sl marker, k to marker, sl marker, m1] twice, k to end. *181[205:229] sts.*

Inc 4 sts on every 4th row as last inc row until 205[229:245] sts, then on every foll 6th row until 221[245:269] sts.

Work straight in st st without shaping until the body measures 24[25:26] cm (9½[9¾:10¼] in) from cast-on edge ending with a p row.

Shape Armholes

Next row: k49[54:59], cast off 12[14:16] sts, k99[109:119], cast off 12[14:16] sts, k to end.

Next row: p49[54:59], p69[75:81] sleeve sts from holder with WSF, p99[109:119], p69[75:81] sleeve sts from other holder with WSF, p across rem 49[54:59] sts. *335[367:399] sts.*

Decrease for armholes as folls:
Row 1: k46[51:56], k2tog, PM, k2, PM, sl1, k1, psso, k63[69:75], k2tog, PM, k2, PM, sl1, k1, psso, k93[103:113], k2tog, PM, k2, PM, sl1, k1, psso, k63[69:75], k2tog, PM, k2, PM, sl1, k1, psso, k to end. *327[359:391] sts.*
Row 2: p.
Row 3: [k to 2 sts before marker, k2tog, sl marker, k2, slip marker, sl1, k1, psso] 4 times, k to end. *319[351:383] sts.*

Row 4: p.
Rep last 2 rows until 223 sts rem, ending with a row 3.

Shape Yoke
Row 1 (WS): k.
Row 2: p.
Row 3: k.
Row 4 (RS): k.
Row 5: p1, [yrn, p2tog] to end of row.
Row 6: k.
Row 7(WS): [k8, k2tog] to last 3 sts, k3. *201 sts.*
Rep rows 2 to 6 once more.

Row 13(WS): [k7, k2tog] to last 3 sts, k3. *179 sts.*
Rep rows 2 to 6 once more.

Row 19 (WS): [k6, k2tog] to last 3 sts, k3. *157 sts.*
Rep rows 2 to 6 once more.

Row 25 (WS): [k5, k2tog] to last 3 sts, k3. *135 sts.*
Rep rows 2 to 6 once more.

Row 31 (WS): [k4, k2tog] to last 3 sts, k3. *113 sts.*
Rep rows 2 to 6 once more.

Two smallest sizes only:
Row 37 (WS): [k3, k2tog] to last 3 sts, k3. *91 sts.*
Rep rows 2 to 6 once more.

All sizes:
Neckband
Change to 3 mm (US 2.5) circs, and work in 1x1 rib as folls:
Row 1: k1, *p1, k1; rep from * to end of row.

Row 2: p1, *k1, p1; rep from * to end of row.
Work 1.5 cm (½ in) in 1x1 rib, ending with a row 2.

Cast (bind) off loosely in rib.

Block lightly to shape.

Join cast-off sections under arms.

Edging
Using a pair of 3 mm (US 2.5) dpns, cast on 9 sts and work a strip of 1x1 rib as long as left front edge, to fit when slightly stretched. Cast off. Attach to left front edge with mattress st.

Make a similar strip of 9 sts in 1x1 rib, making 8 buttonholes at evenly spaced intervals of approx 6[6.5:7] cm (2¼[2½:2¾] in). Attach to right front edge with mattress st.

Sew 8 buttons to left front ribbed edge, corresponding to buttonholes at opposite edge.

Finishing (optional)
Sew tiny beads randomly on to the yoke for a subtle sparkle. Alternatively, embellish the yoke or cuffs more fully by encrusting with diamanté and glass beads for a stunning evening look.

Above: When choosing vintage buttons, it can sometimes be hard to find enough of the same type to finish a garment, so just choose odd ones and make a feature of them. A cheeky flash of colour in the form of mismatching fastenings or beading could liven up the simplicity of this garment.

The Swinging Sixties

Breaking away from the traditional, parent-approved fashions of the previous decade, the 1960s marked a sweeping change in style brought about by the growth of the teen market and prominence of youth culture – hemlines rose dramatically, unisex clothing emerged and the silhouette became A-line rather than hourglass. Even traditional garments, such as the Aran cable-knit sweater, were reworked in the new bold colours of the decade. The knitting projects here exhibit the lively, free approach to colour in the 1960s – a plum and purple mini dress, a striped purse with a polka-dot lining, a tangerine cardigan and a multicoloured Alice band.

Knitting and Fashion

The rather formal daywear, accessorized with matching gloves, bags and shoes, was on the wane by the early 1960s, replaced by a casual spirit of fashion that seemed unbelievably fresh and youthful. Dresses were big news and created in endless variations – the sleeveless shift mini, the empire-waist babydoll, the mini pinafore and the T-shirt dress to name but a few – while the pullover skinny rib was the jumper of choice for student, beatnik and Mod. Geometric motifs borrowed from Pop and Op Art were reworked on knitwear.

Although many knitting booklets at the start of the 1960s included garments that were similar to those from the 1950s, by the middle of the decade the seismic shift that was occurring in style, society and culture could no longer be ignored.

Jerseys moved away from fitted styles, instead featuring little shaping, dropped sleeves and often thicker yarns. Aran knitting became very popular, with booklets showcasing all kinds of cabled styles for the whole family. These were usually knitted in traditional natural cream or undyed shades, but occasionally they came in the bolder colours typical of the era.

Yarn manufacturers embraced the new manmade fibres that were being developed, creating unusual yarns with a metallic sheen and fancy ply, as well as yarns that were moth resistant and easy to care for. For the first time the market was awash with synthetics, and knitters were able to experiment like never before.

Right: Fall fashions of 1961. This boxy mohair sweater and cardigan in punchy yellow and orange, by Jane Irwill, is accessorized with a Liberty scarf.

Key themes

The 1960s saw the epicentre of fashion move from Paris to London, where everything was "swinging" – the music, the cars, the design and of course the clothes. Teenagers, who in the 1950s had begun to reject their parents' style of dress, became a driving force in street style, fashion and consumerism. Many attribute Mary Quant, a leading British designer in the 1960s, for creating the ultimate young person's garment, the ultra-short "mini" skirt, which became an icon of the decade.

Although the popularity of hand-knitting waned slightly, due to increased mass production, there were plenty of patterns for simple, fitted mini dresses and shifts using block colours, lace knitting and ribbing. They were often teamed with matching knee-high socks in bright and colourful colours. Knitting patterns gradually became younger and more fun, with quirky details such as Peter Pan collars, lace cuffs and pockets in contrasting colours. The likes of Twiggy and Joanna Lumley modelled the knits in energetic poses that contrasted dramatically with the staid and serene models of the preceding decades.

Knitted shirt dresses in T-shirt shapes replaced the figure-hugging sweater dresses of the 1950s, while a straight, up-and-down androgenous silhouette replaced the hourglass. Skinny rib sweaters and polo (turtle-) necks were worn under shift dresses or paired with flared jeans. Op and Pop Art trends found resonance in abstract and geometric patterns, either in black and white or in bold, psychedelic colours. Towards the end of the decade, hippy style also influenced knitting patterns: garish colours and lacy crochet became popular, along with longer-length tunics and waistcoats, all styles that continued well into the 1970s.

Above: The actress Susannah York wears a red and yellow striped trapeze mini dress by Deanna Littell for the Mam'selle Boutique in New York, 1967. Exuberant patterns likes these eye-catching stripes worked well when executed in the brash, bright Pop Art colours of the 1960s youth culture.

The Swinging Sixties Mood Board

Clashing colours and swirly patterns, such as hallucinogenic Pucci-style hues and combinations of odd pairings such as apple green and orange, can be worked into many different knitting projects to achieve a 1960s effect. As "space age" materials were also on-trend for the time, consider incorporating metallic threads, plastic discs or shiny fastenings into your work too.

BARBOUR'S
No. 18
SHAMROCK
LINEN
CARPET THREAD
LISBURN, N. IRELAND

Mini Shift Dress

The mini was king in "Swinging London" during the 1960s – both the must-have Mini Cooper car and the tiny skirts first designed mid-decade by Mary Quant. Usually A-line in shape or appearing as a sleeveless shift, the mini dress epitomized the decade and was worn by nearly every woman in the western world. The version here borrows the opulent velvety plum and burgundy colours of the fashion emporium Biba. Barbara Hulanicki, the founder of Biba, as with many of her contemporaries, was inspired by the rich shades of Victorian clothes and design, especially Art Nouveau, and this influence was evident in the era's fashion and design.

Far right: This mini dress can be worn with knee-length boots or flat sandals, however it could also be styled over a turtleneck sweater, colourful opaque tights and some oversized plastic jewellery for a real 1960s Mod look.

YARNS

3[4:4] x 100 g (4 oz) balls of Fyberspates Scrumptious DK, 55% merino wool, 45% silk, 220 m (240 yds) in shade RJ1800, purple (yarn A).

1[1:1] x 100 g (4 oz) balls of Fyberspates Scrumptious DK, 55% merino wool, 45% silk, 220 m (240 yds) in shade 104, plum (yarn B).

Alternative yarns: Any DK or sportweight yarn will work here. The silk and wool mix gives a subtle sheen to the dress, while keeping it warm and cosy. You may want to try a pure silk or cotton for a more summery weight, however, bear in mind that the fabric may be heavier and so stretch more with gravity in the natural way that knitted fabric does.

MEASUREMENTS

Bust

81–86	91–97	102–107 cm
32–34	36–38	40–42 in

Actual Chest

88	99	109 cm
34¾	39	43 in

Hips

91	102	112 cm
36	40	44 in

Length from Shoulder

86	89	92 cm
33¾	35	36¼ in

Armhole

17	19	21 cm
6½	7½	8¼ in

TENSION/GAUGE

20 sts and 24 rows to 10 cm (4 in) in st st using 4 mm (US 6) needles with tension swatch worked in the round.

22 sts and 26 rows to 10 cm (4 in) in twisted cable rib st using 3.5 mm (US 4) needles.

NOTIONS

Pair of 3.5mm (US 4) knitting needles
Pair of 4.5mm (US 7) knitting needles
4 mm (US 6), 80 cm (32 in) long circular needles
3.5 mm (US 4), 80 cm (32 in) long circular needles
Stitch markers, assorted colours
Darning needle

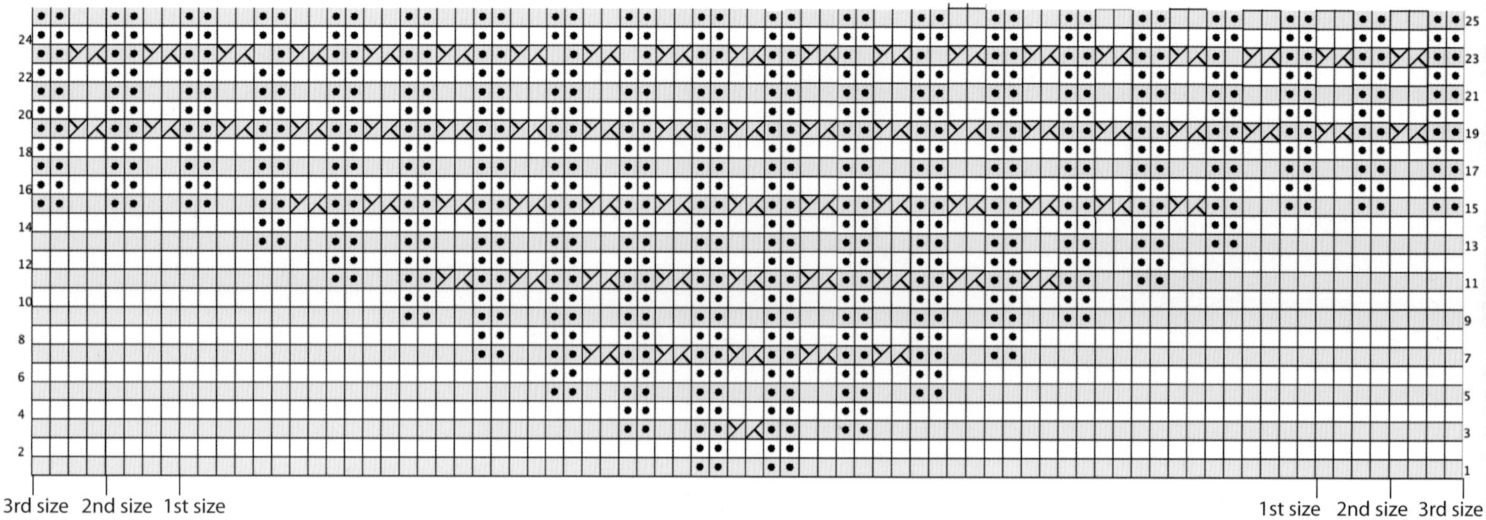

Key

☐ Plain/knit

⊡ Purl

⍂⍁ Twisted Cable

SPECIAL INSTRUCTIONS

Twisted Cable (TC)

Twist 2 = k 2nd st and leave on needle, then k 1st st, slip both off needle.

Twisted Cable Rib (TCR)

Yoke pattern worked in twisted cable rib as per chart (above) – all cables as indicated are twisted cables, all dots are purl ribs.

Hemming

Here the hem is sewn closed as it is much less likely to flip over as you wear it, although you can do a knitted closed hem.

PATTERN

Using 3.5 mm (US 4) circular needles and yarn A, cast on 212[234:254] sts, and join for working in the rnd, PM of first colour at beg of rnd.

Work 7 rnds st st.

Change to 4 mm (US 6) circular needles. **Next row:** p to create hemline.

Cont in st st, dec 4 sts on 14th rnd as folls (placing different coloured markers to that of the beg of rnd marker):

Rnd 14: k25[27:29], PM, sl1, k1, psso, k52[59:65], k2tog, PM, k50[54:58], PM, sl1, k1, psso, k52[59:65], k2tog, PM, k to end. *208[230:250] sts.*

Cont in st st, dec 4 sts on every foll 14th row, until 192[214:234] sts rem, as folls:

Dec row: *k to next marker, sl marker, sl1, k1, psso, k to 2 sts before next marker, k2tog, sl marker; rep from * once more, k to end.

Work straight in st st without dec until work measures 30 cm (11¾ in) from hemline, or 18 cm (7 in) less than desired length-to-waist measurement.

Now decrease for waist, repeating dec row as before on every foll 6th row until 160[182:202] sts rem.

Work straight until work measures 53 [54:55] cm (20¾[21¼:21½] in) from hem.

Increase for bust as folls on next and every foll 7th row until 176[198:218] sts. **Inc row:** *k to next marker, sl marker, m1 by picking up bar, k to next marker, m1, sl marker; rep from * once more, k to end.

Work straight on these 176[198:218] sts until work measures 68[69:70] cm (26¾[27¼:27½] in) from hemline.

Above: To keep the hemline sitting straight, the hem is hand-tacked after the dress is completed, and not knitted in as you work – the latter technique can often cause the hem to flip up in an awkward fashion.

Change to yarn B and cont straight in st st until work measures 69[70:71] cm (27¼[27½:28] in) from hemline or desired length to armhole.

Shape Armholes

Cast off 6[8:8] sts, k 82[90:100], turn and work straight for yoke, leaving rem 88[100:110] sts on holder for back.

NOTE: You may need to change to the 4.5 mm (US 7) needles to keep gauge correct for working straight.

Shape Front

Cast off 6[8:8] sts at beg of next row, then 1 st at either end of every foll row until 62[70:78] sts rem, ending with a p row.

Continue straight for yoke.

Change to 3.5 mm (US 4) needles and begin working yoke pattern as folls:

Row 1: k28[32:36], p2, k2, p2, k to end.

Row 2: p28[32:36], k2, p2, k2, p to end.

Follow the chart opposite for the Twisted Cable Rib pattern – rows 1 and 2 are rows 1 and 2 of chart, cont from these as for chart for relevant size, working 28[32:36] sts either side of first ribs.

Work in rib pattern as set until front measures 12[14:16] cm (4¾[5½:6¼] in), ending with WSR.

Right: Simple shift dresses in the 1960s often had a contrasting colour at the yoke as this knitted one here, however the whole mini could be worked in a block colour to create a versatile and classic piece.

Shape Neck

Patt across 41[46:51] sts, leave last 20[22:24] of these sts on holder for front neck, patt to end.

Work on these 21[24:27] sts in patt for right front.

Dec 1 st at neck edge on every foll row until 11[13:15] sts rem, work straight until armhole measures 17[19:21] cm (6½[7½:8¼] in), ending with a RSR.

Shape Shoulders

Cast off 5[6:7] sts at beg of next row, work one row and cast off rem sts.

Rejoin yarn to rem side and work to match right side, reversing shapings.

Rejoin yarn to 88[100:110] back sts. Cast off 7[9:9] sts at beg of next 2 rows, then dec 1 st at both ends of every foll row until 58[64:72] sts rem.

Cont straight in st st on these sts until armhole measures 17[19:21] cm (6½[7½:8¼] in), ending with a p row.

Cast off 5[6:7] sts at beg of next 4 rows.

Leave rem 38[40:44] sts on holder for the back neck.

Armhole Edging

Using 3.5 mm (US 4) needles and yarn B, rejoin yarn to armhole at shoulder edge of the armhole. With RSF pick up and k87[91:95] sts around the armhole (44[46:48] at the back, 43[45:47] at the front).

Work as folls:
Row 1: k1, *p1, k1 repeat from * to end.
Row 2: p1, *k1, p1 repeat from * to end.
Cast off loosely in rib.

Repeat for second armhole.

Join left shoulder.

Neckline

Using 3.5mm (US 4) needles and yarn B, rejoin yarn to back 38[40:44] sts with RSF and work as folls:
[k2, p2] to last 2[0:0] sts, k2[0:0], pick up 12[12:13] sts along left neck edge, rib 20[22:24] sts from front holder as folls:
k0[0:1], p2[0:2], [k2, p2] to last 2[2:1] sts k2[2:1], pick up 12[12:13] sts along right neck edge.

Work in 2x2 rib on these 82[86:94] sts for 2 rows.

Bind off very loosely.

Finishing

Join rem shoulder seam and sew up hem neatly.

Block all pieces lightly to shape.

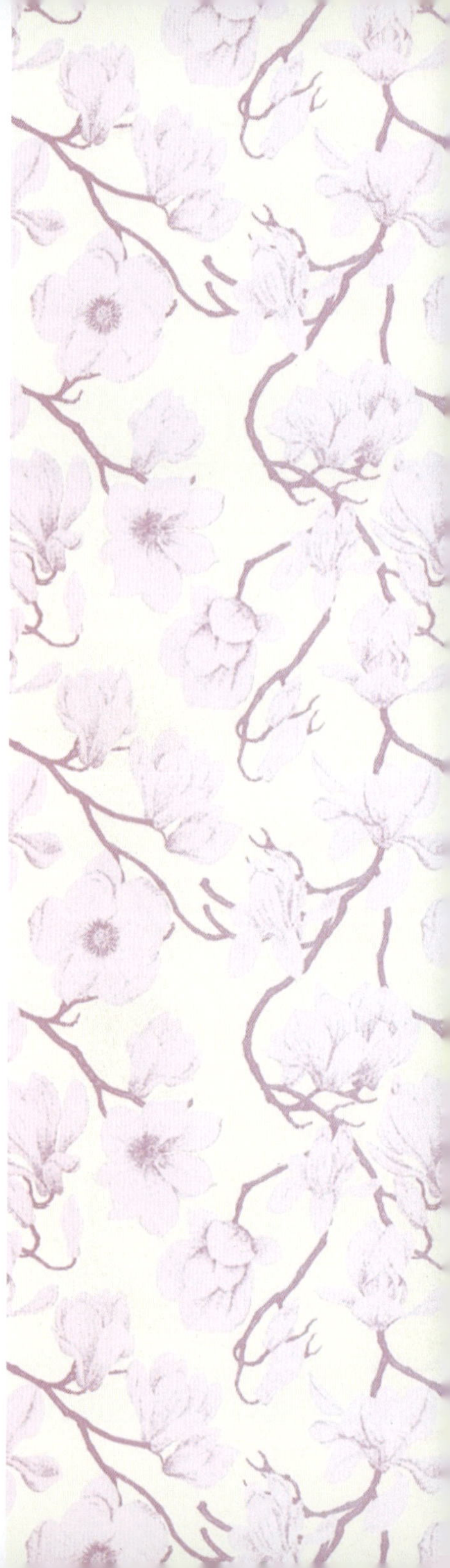

Pucci-Style Purse

The 1960s were a revelation not only in music and freedom but also in fashion and fabrics. This bag takes inspiration from the multicoloured prints and knits of Italian fashion houses Pucci and Missoni, both still going strong today, with much of the same striping, chevrons and stunning multicoloured palettes as resonant now as they once were. Emilio Pucci, known for his jersey loungewear, swimwear and scarves in the 1960s, based his watery colour palette on the hues of the Mediterranean, combining turquoise, coral and emerald in swirls with pinks and yellows.

YARNS
1 x 50 g (2 oz) balls each of Blue Sky Alpacas silk, 50% alpaca, 50% silk, 133 m (145 yds) in: shade 129, amethyst (yarn A), shade 142, lime (yarn B); shade 149 Riviera (yarn C); shade 113, ice (yarn D).

Alternative yarns: Any sportweight or 4-ply yarn can be substituted. If you try other weights of yarn, the bag will just come out larger or smaller accordingly.

MEASUREMENTS
One size, approximately 14 x 14 cm (5½ x 5½ in).

TENSION/GAUGE
25 sts and 32 rows to 10 cm (4 in) in st st using 3.5 mm (US 4) knitting needles.

NOTIONS
Pair of 3.5 mm (US 4) knitting needles
Two 3.25 (US 3) double-pointed needles
Cotton lining fabric, measuring 30 x 16 cm (12 x 6¼ in)
Ready-made purse frame, 9–10 cm (3½–4 in) wide
Darning needle
Needle and thread
All-purpose glue

SPECIAL INSTRUCTIONS
Stripe Pattern
2 rows yarn A
4 rows yarn B
2 rows yarn C
4 rows yarn D
2 rows yarn A
2 rows yarn B
2 rows yarn C
2 rows yarn D
Rep last 8 rows once more
4 more rows yarn D
2 rows yarn A
2 rows yarn B
4 rows yarn C
2 rows yarn D
Rep stripe pattern for length

PATTERN
Using 3.5 mm (US 4) needles, cast on 3 sts.

Work in st st, in stripe pattern above, beg with a p row inc 1 st at both ends of every row until 73 sts.

Next row: dec 1 st at beg of row and inc 1 st at end of row. *73 sts.*

Rep last row 5 times more.

Dec 1 st at both ends of every row until 3 sts rem.

P3tog and fasten off yarn.

Make one further piece in this way.

Block pieces lightly to shape.

Using 3.25 mm (US 3) dpns and yarn D, work a 4 st-wide I-cord of approx 1 m (1 yd) or desired strap length.

Lining
Cut the fabric into two pieces, each measuring 15 x 16 cm (6 x 6¼ in) wide.

Turn under and press a hem of at least 1 cm (½ in) all the way around on each piece.

Sew a piece of fabric to the wrong side of each knitted strip.

Left: Stripes are a fantastic way to add interest and colour to a knitted piece and, when the stripe is turned to a diagonal gradient, even more movement is created in the piece. While recreating a Pucci print would usually call for intricate intarsia patterning, this simple technique retains all the excitement of a busy 1960s textile without complicated techniques.

Right: Use contrasting colours and patterns for the lining and frame to create a very retro-looking purse.

Making Up

Place both strips together with the wrong (lining) sides facing and sew along the bottom and side seams to 3 cm ($1^1/_5$ in) from the top of the purse.

Insert the pouch into the purse frame. If the purse frame has holes for sewing to the fabric, sew the frame into place neatly. Alternatively, use a strong all-purpose glue to attach the frame, and crimp edges into place with pliers for extra security until dry.

Attach the strap to the sides of purse, or if your purse frame has holes or strap hooks, attach them there.

Tangerine Aran Cardigan

Far right: Traditional knits need not be slavishly recreated. Here a time-honoured technique is recreated in a bold colour to great effect. When choosing a colour, ensure it is light enough to allow the cable patterning to be noticeable.

Hand-knitted Aran sweaters were popular with both the young and old in the 1960s. This version is closer-fitting than they were at the time, which gives the sweater a more flattering shape – the bracelet-length sleeve is also very on-trend. Since most people have central heating these days, the pure wool yarn used here is softer and less coarse than the more traditional, hardwearing, straight-off-the-sheep variety traditionally used. Aran sweaters are usually the natural cream colour of undyed wool, but the 1960s saw deliberately clashing hues, such as vibrant tangerine with fuchsia pink. Orange was an iconic colour of the decade, appearing on everything from shag carpets to moulded plastic furniture.

YARN

8[9:10] x 100 g (4 oz) balls of Malabrigo Twist, 100% baby merino wool, 137 m (150 yds) in shade 96, sunset.

Alternative yarns: any worsted weight yarn, but try to keep it as light as possible. Use wool or wool mixes, as Aran knitting uses a lot of yarn and you do not want your cardigan to turn out too heavy and uncomfortable to wear.

MEASUREMENTS

Bust

81–86	91–97	102–107 cm
32–34	36–38	40–42 in

Actual Size

88	102	112 cm
34½	40	44 in

Length from Shoulder

50	54	56 cm
19½	21¼	22 in

Sleeve Seam

41	42	43 cm
16	16½	17 in

Armhole

20	23	25 cm
7¾	9	9¾ in

TENSION/GAUGE

18 sts and 24 rows to 10 cm (4 in) in st st using 5.5 mm (US 9) knitting needles.

23 sts and 24 rows to 10 cm (4 in) across cable patt using 5.5 mm (US 9) knitting needles.

NOTIONS

Pair of 4.5 mm (US 7) knitting needles
Pair of 5.5 mm (US 9) knitting needles
5 x 2 cm (¾ in) diameter leather buttons
Two stitch holders
Darning needle
Cable needle

SPECIAL INSTRUCTIONS

C6B: Cable 6 Back = place next 3 sts onto cn at back of work, k3 from LHN, then k3 from cn.

C6F: Cable 6 Front = place next 3 sts onto cn at front of work, k3 from LHN, then k3 from cn.

C5B: Cable 5 Back = slip next 3 sts onto cn and hold at back of work, knit next 2 sts from LHN, then p1, k2 from the cn

T3B: Twist 3 Back = slip next st onto a cn and leave at back of work. k2, then p1 from cn.

T3F: Twist 3 Front = slip next 2 sts onto a cn and leave at front of work. p1, then k2 from cn.

All ribs are 1x1 unless otherwise stated.

Above: Trinity stitch is a popular choice in traditional Aran sweaters and works well in this weight of yarn. Not as bulky as a bobble stitch; it has a subtle, organic curve.

Trinity Stitch

Row 1(RS): p.
Row 2: *[k1, p1, k1] into next st, p3tog rep from * to end of row.
Row 3: p.
Row 4: *p3tog, [k1, p1, k1] into next st, rep from * to end of row.
Rows 1 to 4 complete pattern, rep for length.

Double Moss Stitch

Row 1: k1, *p1, k1, rep from * to end.
Row 2: p1, *k1, p1, rep from * to end.
Row 3: p1, *k1, p1, rep from * to end.
Row 4: k1, *p1, k1, rep from * to end.
These 4 rows complete pattern, rep for length.

Cable Panel 1 (worked over 13 sts)

Row 1 (RS): T3B, [k1, p1] 3 times, k1, T3F.
Row 2: p2, [k1, p1] 4 times, k1, p2.
Row 3: T3F, [p1, k1] 3 times, p1, T3B.
Row 4: k1, p2, [k1, p1] 4 times, p1, k1.
Row 5: p1, T3F, [p1, k1] twice, p1, T3B, p1.
Row 6: k2, p2, [k1, p1] 3 times, p1, k2.
Row 7: p2, T3F, p1, k1, p1, T3B, p2.
Row 8: k3, p2, k1, p1, k1, p2, k3.
Row 9: p3, T3F, p1, T3B, p3.
Row 10: k4, p2, k1, p2, k4.
Row 11: p4, C5B, p4.
Row 12: As 10th row.
Row 13: p3, T3B, k1, T3F, p3.
Row 14: As 8th row.
Row 15: p2, T3B, k1, p1, k1, T3F, p2.
Row 16: As 6th row.
Row 17: p1, T3B, [k1, p1] twice, k1, T3F, p1.
Row 18: As 4th row.
These 18 rows form panel 1 patt.

Cable Panel 2 (worked over 6 sts)

Row 1(RS): k.
Row 2: p.
Row 3: C6F.
Work 3 rows st st, beg with p row.
Row 7: C6F.
Rep rows 4 to 7 for this panel.

Cable Panel 3 (worked over 6 sts)

Row 1(RS): k.
Row 2: p.
Row 3: C6B.
Work 3 rows st st, beg with p row.
Row 7: C6B.
Rep rows 4 to 7 for this panel.

PATTERN

Back

Using 4.5 mm (US 7) needles, cast on 101[117:129] sts and work 5 cm (2 in) in 1x1 rib ending with a WSR, increasing 1 st on last row. *102[118:130] sts.*

Change to 5.5 mm (US 9) needles and cont in pattern as folls, starting all panels/stitches from row 1:
Row 1(RS): double moss across 9[17:23] sts, p1, panel 1, p1, k1, p1, panel 2, p1, k1, p1, trinity stitch across 32 sts, p1, k1, p1, panel 3, p1, k1, p1, panel 1, p1, double moss across 9[17:23] sts.
Row 2: double moss across 9[17:23] sts, k1, panel 1, k1, p1, k1, panel 32, k1, p1, k1, trinity stitch across 32 sts, k1, p1, k1, panel 2, k1, p1, k1, panel 1, k1, double moss across 9[17:23] sts.

Rep these 2 rows until work measures 30[31:31] cm (11¾[12¼:12¼] in), ending with a WSR.

Left: A mixture of different cables and ribs are used in Aran knitting. To guarantee that you like the tension of each technique in your chosen yarn, ensure that you swatch thoroughly before you begin.

Beg dec for raglan sleeves as folls, cont pattern as established:
Next row: cast off 5[7:8] sts at beg of next two rows. *92[104:114] sts.*
Row 1: k2, sl1, k1, psso, patt to last 4 sts, k2tog, k2.
Row 2: p2, patt to last 2 sts, p2.
Keeping patt correct as long as possible, rep last 2 rows until 46[50:54] sts rem, ending with a row 2.

Cast off all sts.

Left Front

Using 4.5 mm (US 7) needles, cast on 55[63:69] sts and work 5 cm (2 in) in 1x1 rib ending with a WSR, increasing 1st on last row. *56[64:70] sts.*

Change to 5.5 mm (US 9) needles and cont in patt as folls, beg each panel and stitch pattern from row 1:
Row 1: double moss over 9[17:23] sts, p1, k1, p1, panel 1, p1, k1, p1, panel 2, p1, k1, p1, trinity st 8 sts, k1, [p1, k1] 5 times.
Row 2: [p1, k1] 5 times, p1, trinity stitch over 8 sts, k1, p1, k1, panel 2, k1, p1, k1, panel 1, k1, p1, k1, double moss to end.

Rep until work measures 30[31:31] cm (11¾[12¼:12¼] in), ending with a WSR.

Beg dec for raglan sleeves as folls, keeping pattern as established:
Next row: cast off 5[7:8] sts at beg of next row. *51[57:62] sts.*
Row 1: pattern to last 2 sts, p2.
Row 2: k2, sl1, k1, psso, patt to end.
Keeping patt correct as long as possible, rep last 2 rows until 34[36:38] sts rem, ending with a WSR.

Shape Neck

While cont in pattern, decreasing as established at raglan shoulder, shape neck as folls:
Next row: work to last 10 rib sts, place these 10 sts onto a holder. Turn.

Right: A raglan sleeve always looks pretty, and with Aran fabric tending to the bulky side, the fully-fashioned seam eliminates any clumsy joining. Use a mattress stitch to ensure the seam is even tidier.

Far right: The button choice here is a modern reproduction of classic leather buttons, which were often paired with traditional Aran designs. This reference to the past means the modern colour choice is less jarring. A modern button would, of course, work just as well.

Next row: cast off next 12[14:16] sts, patt to end.

While cont to dec at raglan, dec 1 st at neck edge of every other row until 2 sts rem. P2tog and fasten off.

Dec at outer edge of raglan when there are insufficient sts to work within border.

Right Front

Using 4. 5mm (US 7) needles, cast on 55[63:69] sts and work 2 cm (¾ in) 1x1 rib ending with a WSR.

Buttonhole row: rib 3 sts, cast off next 3 sts, rib to end.
Next row: rib to buttonhole, cast on three sts, rib to end.

Cont in rib as before buttonhole until work measures 5 cm (2 in) from cast-on edge, ending with a WSR, increasing 1 st on last row. *56[64:70] sts.*

Change to 5.5 mm (US 9) needles and cont in pattern as folls, beg each panel and stitch pattern from row 1:
Row 1: [k1, p1] 5 times, k1, trinity st over 8 sts, p1, k1, p1, panel 3, p1, k1, p1, panel 1, p1, k1, p1, double moss to end.
Row 2: double moss over 9[17:23]sts, k1, p1, k1, panel 1, k1, p1, k1, panel 3, k1, p1, k1, trinity st 8 sts, p1, [k1, p1] 5 times.
Rep until 24[30:32] rows have been worked from last buttonhole.
Buttonhole row: rib 3 sts, cast off next 3 sts, patt to end.
Next row: patt to buttonhole, cast on 3 sts, rib to end.

Rep patt as established, working 3 more buttonholes on every 27th[29th:31st] row until front measures 30[31:31] cm (11¾[12¼:12¼] in), ending with a RSR.

Beg dec for raglan sleeves as folls:
Next row: cast off 5[7:8] sts at beg of next row. *51[57:62] sts.*
Row 1: patt to last 4 sts, k2tog, k2.
Row 2: p2, pattern to end.
Keeping pattern correct as long as possible, and working buttonholes as established, rep last 2 rows until 34 [36:38] sts rem, ending with a RSR.

Shape Neck

While cont in pattern, decreasing as established at raglan shoulder, shape neck as folls:
Next row: patt to last 10 rib sts, place these 10 sts onto a holder. Turn.
Next row: cast off next 12[14:16] sts sts, patt to end.
While cont to dec at raglan, dec 1 st at neck edge of every other row until 2 sts rem. P2tog and fasten off.

Sleeves

Using 4.5 mm (US 7) needles, cast on 51[55:57] sts and work work 5 cm (2 in) in 1x1 rib ending with a WSR, increasing 1 st on last row. *52[56:58] sts.*

Change to 5.5 mm (US 9) needles.
Row 1(RS): double moss across 2[4:5] sts, panel 3, p1, panel 3, p1, k1, p1, trinity st over 16 sts, p1, k1, p1, panel 2, p1, panel 2, double moss to end.
Row 2: double moss across 2[4:5] sts, panel 2, k1, panel 2, k1, p1, k1, trinity st over 16 sts, k1, p1, k1, panel 3, k1, panel 3, double moss to end.

Cont in patt as established, increasing 1 st at either end of 11th[11th:3rd] row and every foll 10th[6th:6th] row until there are 66[78:86] sts, bringing extra sts into double moss patt.
Work straight until sleeve measures 41[42:43] cm (16[16½:17] in) from cast-on edge, ending with a WSR.

Beg dec for raglan sleeves as folls, keeping patt as established:
Next row: cast off 5[7:8] sts at beg of next 2 rows. *56[64:70] sts.*
Row 1: k2, sl1, k1, psso, patt to last 4 sts, k2tog, k2.
Row 2: p2, patt to last 2 sts, p2.
Keeping patt correct as long as possible, rep last 2 rows until 10 sts rem, ending with row 2. Cast off all sts.

Making Up

Join raglan seams, then sew up side and underarm seams in one long seam at either side.

Neckband

With RSF, using 4.5 mm (US 7) needles, attach yarn to 10 sts on holder at right front, rib across these 10 sts, pick up and k 10[12:14] sts from right front neck, pick up 8 sts from shoulder, 45[49:53] sts from back neck, 8 from shoulder, 10[12:14] down left front and rib 10 from rem holder. *101[109:117] sts.*

Turn and work in 1x1 rib on these 101[109:117] sts for 2 further rows.
Next row: rib to last 6 sts, cast off 3 sts, rib to end.
Next row: rib 3 sts, cast on 3 sts, rib to end.
Work 2 further rows in rib without buttonholes. Cast off in rib.
Sew on buttons.

Multicoloured Alice Band

The simple hairband was ubiquitous in the 1960s, whether made in pastel colours and worn over long hair with a fringe on little girls and teenyboppers, thick and bold over a blunt bob haircut on the Mods and Beats, or as a multicoloured, fringed and beaded "flower power" headband for hippies. This version can be worn to tie the hair out of the face or across the forehead as a colourful fashion statement.

YARN
1 x 50 g (2 oz) ball of Koigu KPPPM, 100% merino wool, 160 m (175 yds) in shade P118.

Alternative yarns: Any sock weight or 4-ply yarn will substitute here.

MEASUREMENTS
One size, approximately 9 cm (3¾ in) wide to fit average adult head.

TENSION/GAUGE
28 sts to 10 cm (4 in) in moss (seed) st using 3 mm (US 2.5) knitting needles.

NOTIONS
Pair of 3 mm (US 2.5) knitting needles
Two 2.5 mm (US 1) double-pointed needles
Darning needle

SPECIAL INSTRUCTIONS
Moss (Seed) Stitch
Row 1: k1*p1, k1, rep from * to end. This row forms patt.

PATTERN
Using 2.5 mm (US 1) dpns, cast on 4 sts and work an I-cord of approx 50 cm (19½ in), or to desired length.

Change to 3 mm (US 2.5) straight needles and knit across 4 sts, inc 1 in last st. *5 sts.*

Next row: work in moss (seed) st, inc 1 st at both ends of row. *7 sts.*
Rep last row until there are 25 sts.

Work straight in moss (seed) st for 20 cm (7¾ in).
Next row: work in moss (seed) st, dec 1 st at both ends of row. *23 sts.*
Rep last row until there are 5 sts.
k1 row, dec 1 st at end of row. *4 sts.*

Change to 2.5 mm (US 1) dpns and work an I-cord of approx 50 cm (19½ in), or to desired length on these 4 sts. Cast (bind) off all sts.

Above and right: A simple stitch and design can be made into a stunning accessory by choosing a pretty mulitcoloured hand-dyed yarn.

The Groovy Seventies

The decade began with the continuation of hippy "Summer of Love" fashions – peasant clothing with fringes, beading, ethnic embroidery and lacings, super-long maxis and hipsters worn with big belts. Nostalgia was another theme, seen in Edwardian influences from Laura Ashley and floppy hats and long granny dresses from Biba, while the disco craze toward the end of the decade led to clingy jersey dresses, tube tops, lurex haltertops and jumpsuits. Everything was loose, unstructured and comfortable, making the styles of the day easy to replicate in knitwear. To create a retro feel for the projects on the following pages, earthy colours of yarn have been chosen, though you may prefer to substitute more fashionable colours for a modern look.

Knitting and Fashion

Along with high fashion knitwear from Sonia Rykiel, Kenzo and Missoni, there were artist-knitters such as Adrienne Toth Vittadini, John Ashpool, Bill Gibb and Kaffe Fassett who had a huge influence on home knitters. The expression of artistic creativity in knitting became an important idea that inspired the burgeoning craft market, with designers drawing on themes from the natural world, popular culture and ethnic sources such as Eastern textiles and Native American and Aztec patterns.

The 1970s are often referred to as the decade that taste forgot, and many of the garish shapeless knits from the era seem to back up this claim. The fashions were for bold and clashing colours, textures and prints, often worn in layers. However, the Italian fashion giant Missoni succeeded in working these colours and textures into their knitwear in an extremely elegant way, influencing knitting patterns by inspiring crisp chevrons and candy stripes as well as long-length cardigans and skirts.

The fashion for a more hippy, bohemian and natural way of life saw knitting re-emerge as a popular craft. Handcrafts, such as knitting, crochet, patchwork, découpage and macramé, became all the rage, with housewives producing everything from knotted plant-pot holders and crochet net curtains to patchwork quilts. This reawakening of crafts saw a surge in handicraft books, alongside more traditional knitting-

Right: Co-ordinating stripy ensembles by Mary Quant from 1975 are topped off by extra-long *Dr Who*-style scarves and matching beanies.

based booklets. *Stitchcraft* was still going strong, but it began to feature other crafts and not just knitting.

Key themes

The 1970s were all about choice, which meant you could find a knitting pattern for almost anything, from a bikini to a full-length evening gown. Glitzy halter and cropped tops, hotpants, tight skullcaps and long scarves were all popular, and the poncho and shawl were featured in almost every knitting compilation. These were often heavily patterned, an effect that was achieved with colourwork, stripes and embroidery. The hippie movement spawned folksy, ethnic pieces such as kaftans, tunics and fringed waistcoats.

Towards the end of the decade, a less bohemian, more feminine, Laura Ashley style began to emerge. Patterns for sweaters were often lacy and knitted in light colours, and featured high collars and puffed sleeves. In a move away from the knitting designers of the past, who contributed to publications like *Vogue Knitting*, certain hand-knitters started to become well known for their designs. Bill Gibb, for example, reworked Fair Isle and Aran into voluminous and dramatic pieces, while California-born Kaffe Fassett, who worked in fabulous colours and geometric shapes, had a massive influence on the knitting palette of the 1970s and 1980s, and is still designing today.

Above: Knitwear was an essential feature of the homespun back-to-nature movement of the 1970s when anything craft-oriented and home-grown was idealized. Here brimmed hats are worn with a sweater dress and stripy jumper and skirt. For a floppy version of the hat, see pages 126–9.

The Groovy Seventies Mood Board

Relaxed and free-flowing, knitwear was inspired largely by the "back-to-nature" movement. Earth colours in peach, brown and yellow abounded, although Laura Ashley made a statement with pastel paisley and florals while Biba was known for the "Auntie" shades of plum, rust and berry. Fringing, hippie beads and feathers all could be used to add a suitably retro touch to knitwear.

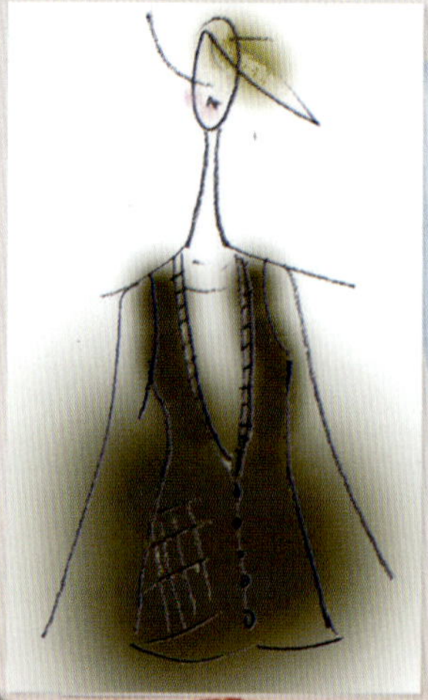

Rose Petal by Patricia Roberts

Plain Dealing by Patricia Roberts

Floppy Sunhat

The bohemian, flowing "flower power" maxi dress of the early 1970s was frequently topped with a floppy-brimmed, often felt, hat, perched on top of long, sunkissed locks… or sometimes it was seen teamed with a Biba-style mini dress or on the beach with a knitted bikini! Here, the silk yarn used lends a stylish sheen and the wire inserted into the edge does all the work of holding the brim away from the face: a perfect hat for a summer music festival!

YARN

4 x 30 g (1 oz) balls of Shilasdair Cord Silk, 100% silk, 70 m (77 yds) in shade a3.

Alternative yarns: any sportweight or light DK weight yarn. You could also try a wool yarn and lightly felt it to get a more authentic period look.

MEASUREMENTS

One size, approximately 36 cm (14 in) in diameter across brim, to fit the average adult head.

TENSION/GAUGE

24 sts and 32 rows to 10 cm (4 in) in st st using 3.75 mm (US 5) knitting needles.

Left: Knitted hats are not just for winter; this beautiful silk sunhat is light enough to be worn on the hottest of days with a sundress and flip-flops. If you prefer warm hats, work it in a wool yarn and felt it for a cosy, stiff-brimmed, all-weather hat.

NOTIONS

Set of 4 x 3.75 mm (US 5) double-pointed needles or circular needle
Darning needle
Sewing needle and thread
Light jewellery or millinery wire

PATTERN

Work as one piece and start at the brim.

Brim

Using a set of four 3.75 mm (US 5) needles, cast on 250 sts. Distribute the stitches over the needles and position for working in the rnd. PM at beg of the rnd and slip the marker at the beg of every rnd.

Rnd 1 to 4: k.
Rnd 5: * k8, k2tog; rep from * to end.
225 sts.
k3 rnds.
Rnd 9: * k7, k2tog; rep from * to end.
200 sts.
k 5 rnds.
Rnd 15: * k6, k2tog; rep from * to end.
175 sts.
k5 rnds.
Rnd 21: * k5, k2tog; rep from * to end.
150 sts.
k5 rnds.
Rnd 27:* k4, k2tog; rep from * to end.
125 sts.
Rnd 28: k.
Brim completed.

Crown

Rnd 1: [yfwd, k2tog] to end of rnd, ending last rep k3tog. *124 sts.*
Rnd 2: k.
Rnd 3: [yfwd, k2tog] to end of rnd.
Rep last two rnds for approx 6 cm (2¼ in).
Work straight in st st until crown measures approx 12 cm (4¾ in).

Shape Crown

Rnd 1: [k6, k2tog] 14 times, k6, k3tog, k3. *108 sts.*
Rnd 2 and every alternate rnd: k.
Rnd 3: [k7, k2tog] 12 times. *96 sts.*
Rnd 5: [k6, k2tog] 12 times. *84 sts.*
Rnd 7: [k5, k2tog] 12 times. *72 sts.*
Rnd 9: [k4, k2tog] 12 times. *60 sts.*
Rnd 11: [k3, k2tog] 12 times. *48 sts.*
Rnd 13: [k2, k2tog] 12 times. *36 sts.*
Rnd 14: [k1, k2tog] 12 times. *24 sts.*
Rnd 16: [k2tog] 12 times. *12 sts.*
Cut yarn and thread through rem sts and pull tightly to gather. Fasten off.

Finishing

Block hat lightly and sew wire all round the edge of the brim, folding a small hem around the wire and sewing neatly into place.

Use a cord or ribbon (or a twisted cord in a complementary yarn) to thread in and out of the lace border, along the join where the brim meets the crown. Tie in a bow and tighten to fit the head, as desired.

Above: This yarn twist tie adds a country charm to the hat. For a pretty summer bonnet look, thread a wide ribbon through the hat instead, leaving long, loose ties on the bow.

"Summer of Love" Waistcoat

Far right: The waistcoat has had a renaissance in recent years. Fantastic for layering over tees, shirts or dresses, this long-line version could be worn with jeans, leggings or a maxi dress for a comfortable yet smart look.

Waistcoats were all the rage in the 1970s, with everyone from hippies to middle-aged housewives and even glam rockers wearing them. Worn long with flares and platforms and often crocheted in garish colours, this wasn't a look for the faint-hearted! This version is long yet streamlined and created in one colour with knit and purl detailing to add texture. The racerback is a modern twist and allows the waistcoat to be worn layered over skinny tops or alone as a buttoned-up vest.

YARN

7[8:9] x 50 g (2 oz) balls of Artesano Alpaca DK yarn, 100% pure superfine alpaca, 100 m (109 yds) in shade 33, brown.

Alternative yarns: any DK weight yarn is perfect. If you want the patterning to stand out more, work it in a crisp wool or light-coloured yarn.

MEASUREMENTS

Bust

81–86	91–97	102–107 cm
32–34	36–38	40–42 in

Actual Size

87	98	109 cm
34¼	38½	43 in

Length

70	72	74 cm
27½	28¼	29 in

Armhole

20	21	23 cm
7¾	8¼	9 in

TENSION/GAUGE

22 sts and 30 rows to 10 cm (4 in) in st st using 4 mm (US 6) knitting needles.

NOTIONS

Pair of 3.5 mm (US 4) knitting needles
Pair of 4 mm (US 6) knitting needles
6 x 1 cm (½ in) diameter buttons
Darning needle

PATTERN

Back

Using 3.5 mm (US 4) needles, cast on 106[118:130] sts and work in 2x2 rib as folls:

Row 1: k2, *p2, k2; rep from * to end of row.

Row 2: p2, *k2, p2; rep from * to end of row.

Rep these 2 rows until work measures 7 cm (3¾ in), ending with a row 2.

Change to 4 mm (US 6) needles and st st and work straight until work measures 16 cm (6¼ in) from cast-on edge, ending with a p row.

Shape Waist

Dec 1 st at either end of next and every foll 4th row until 86[98:110] sts rem.

Work 7 rows straight in st st without decreasing.

Inc 1 st at either end of next and every foll 6th row until 96[108:120] sts.

Work straight until work measures 50[51:51] cm (19¾[20:20] in) from cast-on edge, ending with a p row.

Shape Armholes and Racerback
Cast off 8[9:9] sts at beg of next 2 rows. *80[90:102] sts.*

Now cast off 2 sts at beg of next 4 rows, then dec 1 st at both ends of every foll row 9[9:10] times, then every foll alt row 7 times. *40[50:60] sts.*

Work straight in st st without decreasing for 4[5:6] cm (1½[2:2¼] in) ending with a p row.

Inc 1 st at either end of next and every foll alt row 4 times in all, then every foll row 5 times, then cast on 2 sts at beg of next 4 rows. *66[76:86] sts.*

Work straight until work measures 20 [21:23] cm (7¾[8¼:9] in) from beg of armhole shaping, ending with a p row.

Shape Shoulders
Cast off 6[7:9] sts at beg of next two rows, cast off 5[7:8] sts at beg of foll two rows, cast off rem 44[48:52] sts.

Left Front
Cast on 50[58:62] sts and work in 2x2 rib as folls:
Row 1: k2, *p2, k2; rep from * to end of row.
Row 2: p2, *k2, p2; rep from * to end of row.

Rep these 2 rows until work measures 7 cm (3¾ in), ending with a row 2.

Change to 4 mm (US 6) needles and work in patt as folls until work measures 16 cm (6¼ in) from cast-on edge, ending with a WSR:
Row 1: k2, *p4, k4; rep from * to last 0[0:4] sts, p4.
Row 2: k0[0:4]*p4, k4; rep from * to last 2 sts, p2.
Rep last 2 rows once more.
Next row: p2, *k4, p4; rep from * to last 0[0:4] sts, k4.
Next row: p0[0:4]*k4, p4; rep from * to last 2 sts, k2.
Rep last 2 rows once more.
These 8 rows form pattern, rep for front.

Shape Waist

Maintaining continuity of pattern, shape for the waist as folls:
Dec 1 st at beg of next and every foll 4th row until 40[48:52] sts rem.

Work 7 rows straight in pattern without decreasing.

Inc 1 st at beg of next row and every foll 6th row 5 times, while at the same time, dec 1 st at neck edge of next and every foll 6th row.

Once 5 waist increases have been worked, work straight at side edge until work measures 50[51:51] cm (19¾[20:20] in) from cast-on edge, ending with a WSR, while at the same time, continuing to dec 1 st at neck edge of every 6th[4th:4th] row.

Cast off 8[9:9]sts at beg of next row.

Dec 1 st at armhole edge of every foll row 3 times, then every foll alt row 4 times.

Work straight at armhole, while at the same time, continuing to dec 1 st at neck edge of every 6th[4th:4th] row until 11[14:17] sts rem.

Work straight on these sts until armhole measures same as back to shoulder shaping, ending with a p WSR.

Cast off 6[7:9] sts at beg of next row.
Next row: work in patt.
Cast off rem 5[7:8] sts.

Right Front

Work as left front, reversing all shapings.

Finishing

Press all pieces lightly.
Join shoulder seams.

Arm edgings

Pick up and k 103[107:113] sts evenly around armhole edges and work 4 rows 1x1 rib on these sts.

Cast off loosely in rib.

Neckband

Cast on 7 sts and work in 1x1 rib on these sts for 4 rows, work a buttonhole on next and every foll 16th row until you have 6 buttonholes, as folls:
Buttonhole row: k1, p1, k1, yfwd, k2tog, p1, k1.

Cont straight in rib until strip is long enough to fit all around neck edge. Cast off all sts.

Sew neckband to neck edge neatly, with buttonholes at bottom right front.

Sew 6 buttons at bottom left front of neckband to correspond to buttonholes.

Far left top:
Racerback vests were the inspiration for the deep armholes in this pattern, which gives the waistcoat a modern feel and adds interest to an otherwise plain back.

Far left bottom:
Choosing vintage buttons to use in a piece is great fun and this waistcoat is such a simple classic that you can choose quirky and colourful buttons, if you so wish.

Extra-Long Stripy Scarf

It seems that in the 1970s, a scarf could not be called a scarf unless it was 3 m (10 ft) long, bright and stripy! So here is a version with the Missoni-style striped pattern made more interesting using a feather and fan stitch and a grown-up, muted palette. The yarn chosen here is hand-dyed using natural sources such as onion skins and indigo, which creates a subtle colour range. Of course, you can make the scarf shorter and more manageable, and it is also an ideal project for using up stash yarn – you could make each stripe a different yarn and end up with a true *Doctor Who*-style scarf.

YARNS

1 x 100 g (4 oz) ball each of Shilasdair Luxury DK, 20% cashmere, 40% angora, 40% British merino lambswool, 300 m (330 yd) in shade v, spring forest (yarn A); shade c, tansy gold (yarn B) and shade e, light brown (yarn C).

Alternative yarns: Use any sportweight or DK yarn to achieve the same-sized scarf. If you try different yarns, the resulting scarf will just come out smaller or larger, accordingly. Try scraps of yarn from your stash or left over from other patterns in this book for a colourful and textured project.

Below: The classic "feather and fan" lace pattern naturally creates a scalloped edge, which is the perfect detail for an overlong scarf.

MEASUREMENTS

One size. Scarf measures approximately 18 cm (7 in) in width and 4 m (13 ft) in length.

TENSION/GAUGE

21 sts and 22 rows to 10 cm (4 in) in pattern using 4.5 mm (US 7) knitting needles.

NOTIONS

4.5 mm (US 7) knitting needles
Darning needle

SPECIAL INSTRUCTIONS

Feather and Fan Stitch

Row 1: k.
Row 2: p.
Row 3: k1 *[k2tog] 3 times, [yo, k1] 6 times [k2tog] 3 times; rep from * to last st k1.
Row 4: k.
Rep these 4 rows for the pattern.

PATTERN

Using yarn A and 4.5 mm (US 7) needles, cast on 38 sts.
Work in feather and fan stitch for entire scarf, changing colour every 8 rows until the scarf is the desired length…or your yarn runs out!

Weave in all ends and block lightly.

Above: Striping within this particular lace pattern gives pleasing wavy lines, creating movement and texture with little effort. Try even more colours for a really eye-catching piece.

Right: Part of the fun of such a long scarf is to wind it around the neck many times in an attractive pile, although of course it can easily be knitted shorter for a more practical accessory.

Easy Poncho Wrap

At the height of popularity in the 1970s, the poncho was most often knitted or crocheted in styles that slipped over the head, and worn with huge bellbottom jeans. Traditionally designed as a diamond-shaped with a central opening and in ethnic styles with fringing, this adaptation is far more grown-up and understated. Constructed as a simple split rectangle, it is a combination of a classic poncho and a cape that will keep you warm yet look elegant. The poncho can be worn loose as a shoulder wrap or cinched in with a belt high at the waist.

YARN

3 x 100 g (4 oz) balls of Malabrigo Sock, 100% superwash merino, 402 m (440 yds) in shade 851, turner.

Alternative yarns: Any sockweight or 4-ply yarn will substitute here, but as the wrap is not fitted, you could try slight variations on weights to result in a slightly larger or smaller version.

MEASUREMENTS

One size, approximately 102 cm (40¼ in) long and 81 cm (31¾ in) wide.

TENSION/GAUGE

20 sts and 26 rows to 10 cm (4 in) in pattern using 4 mm (US 6) knitting needles.

NOTIONS

Pair of 4 mm (US 6) knitting needles
Darning needle

TIP: You may wish to knit this on a circular needle to hold the weight of all the stitches.

Left: A space-dyed yarn is always attractive, however, the basketweave technique would stand out even more using a solid or semi-solid colour.

Right: You can wear this wrap in many ways – belted like a poncho, hanging loose like a shawl or casually wrapped around the neck like a stole or scarf. It makes a great piece for spring or autumn when you may not need a heavy coat.

Above: The wrap has a neat garter stitch border to ensure all edges of the wrap lay flat and even.

PATTERN

Using 4 mm (US 6) needles, cast on 162 sts and work and work 10 rows in garter stitch. Now proceed in patt as folls:

Rows 1 to 6: k5, [k4, p4] to last 5 sts, k5.

Row 7 to 12: k5, [p4, k4] to last 5 sts, k5.

Repeat last 12 rows of pattern until work measures 48 cm (19 in) ending with a WSR.

Next row: k5, pattern over 72 sts, k4 for front band, leave rem sts on a holder.

Next row: k4, pattern over 72 sts, k5.

Repeat these 2 rows until work measures 54 cm (21¼ in) from divider row, then work 10 rows garter stitch. Cast off loosely.

With RSF, join yarn to other side, then work as folls:

Next row: k4, patt over 72 sts, k5.

Next row: k5, patt over 72 sts, k4.

Continue working these 2 rows until work measures the same as the other side to the garter border, then work 10 rows garter stitch.

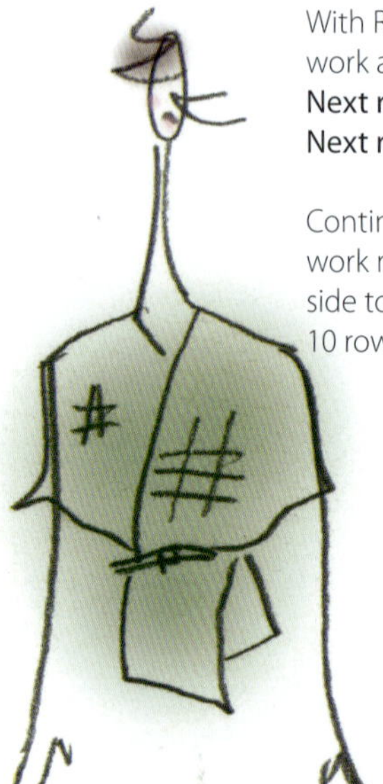

Cast off loosely.

Block lightly to shape.

The Dramatic Eighties

High-luxe, extravagant and theatrical, the 1980s were a period of assertive attitudes and bold colours. Fashion-wise, the triangle inverted from the 1970s – instead of loose skirts and trousers worn with skinny tops, voluminous jumpers and blouses were paired with bodycon leggings and Lycra mini skirts. Everything was oversized: from massive shoulderpads to off-the-shoulder slouchy sweaters, it was all big, big, big, and not just in Japan.

On the following pages are a pick of the many well-loved 1980s trends – the oversized mohair jumper and legwarmers tap into the decade's dancewear obsession, the metallic batwing is all about gold and glitz, while the cropped cable-knit and fingerless gloves have a Madonna-inspired feel.

Knitting and Fashion

With the influence of MTV, pop fashion styles were quick to translate to the rest of the world – crazy mismatching patterns, such as florals with tartans, stripes or checks, were enthusiastically embraced, as were bold neons and colour blocks, animal prints, intarsia and graffiti-inspired designs. *Dynasty* and *Working Girl* offered up power-dressing and ostentatious jewellery, while *Flashdance* and Jane Fonda inspired the dancewear-to-streetwear fad.

Right: Soft, fluffy knits in luxury fibres were a classic 1980s trend. Here a long grey angora sweater-jacket is worn with a pearlized pewter leather skirt in 1981. Shoulder pads and a wide neckline give the piece a big-shouldered *Dynasty* feel.

The revival in hand-knitting, which began in the 1970s, continued into the 1980s due to the cheap availability of manmade yarns compared with the price of ready-made garments. Mohair and mohair mixes were popular, and the fibre of choice with the alternative punk scene of the late 1970s and early 1980s. At this time the consensus was "the fuzzier the better", so many jumpers had a substantial halo of hair that contributed to the already outsized shape. Punks, although anarchic and rebellious, also took up handcrafting out of necessity, by ripping and customizing their clothes in order to get the "look". They also knitted their own misshapen, baggy and laddered mohair jumpers on large needles. By the mid 1980s this style and technique had influenced mainstream knitting patterns, with lace and transparent fabrics being produced in an echo of the more random open-knit versions of the punk era.

Kaffe Fassett continued to be an influential knitwear designer in the 1980s, producing oversized sweaters, throws and coat-style cardigans in complicated patterns using myriad vibrant shades that almost seemed to dance. The decade was also about texture, not only with mohair, but also with novelty and fancy yarns and knitted bobbles, raised stitches, loops and cables. Patricia Roberts – another big name in the world of 1980s knitwear – produced fun patterns in bright colours and using intarsia bow motifs, bobbles and Fair Isle to create a zany yet cute style. With her books and television appearances in the US, Elizabeth Zimmerman encouraged knitters outside of Scandinavia to knit in the Continental style and work in the round, often making jumpers in one piece – a tradition that continues today.

Left: Brooke Shields does for legwarmers what she did for Calvin Klein jeans: here she layers chunky warmers with a bobbly pattern over stripy tights in 1983.

Key themes

The New Romantics brought in lots of leather and lace detailing, frilled pirate-style shirts and ruffled ra-ra skirts while punk fashioning still reigned supreme with safety pin-pierced and ripped T-shirts and sweatshirts galore. The batwing sleeve was a particularly popular style. It was a throwback to the dolman sleeves of the 1950s, a decade that had a massive influence on 1980s fashion. Other 1950s-inspired details included furry yarns, such as angora (or manmade equivalents), pastel colours and intarsia bow motifs – often all of these were included in one jumper! The silhouette continued to be oversized, like the hairstyles of the time, with dropped shoulders, a positive ease of at least 10 cm (4 in) and shaping reserved for the ribbed cuffs and edgings.

Intarsia "picture" jumpers were also big news, with brands such as Krizia and Joseph Tricot inspiring knitters to try home-made versions – large-scale motifs were preferred, from classical sculpture or art to animals and abstracts. Lavishly beaded, sequinned and appliquéd knitwear took a turn as sumptuous eveningwear, while preppy cable-knits were paired with pretty lace collars for an all-American look.

The Dramatic Eighties Mood Board

Texture, pattern and colour mixes were an over-riding feature of 1980s fashion, so consider combining crazy fluro colours such as pink, orange or turquoise with black to make them "pop" and using stripes and colour blocks together. For flashy retro detailing, you might like to use large gold logo buttons for your knitwear, embellish your pieces with appliqué or sequins or incorporate loops or bobbles to add surface texture.

Columbine by Patricia Roberts

Calamity by Patricia Roberts

Glittery Batwing Sweater

The 1950s was a huge influence on fashion in the 1980s, and the dolman sleeve was reinvented in an exaggerated, theatrical manner to become what we know as the "batwing". A true batwing has an armhole opening that extends almost to the waist, with a sleeve that then tapers to the wrist, but this adaptation features a slightly less dramatic sleeve – one that is reined in again to halfway between the dolman and the batwing. Because luxury, sparkle and drama were sought-after effects in this decade, the yarn chosen has a subtle sheen with a touch of lurex, creating an elegant, yet stunning piece that would be perfect for eveningwear.

YARN

9[10:11] x 50 g (2 oz) balls of Karabella Glimmer, 90% rayon, 10% lurex, 128 m (141 yds) in shade 676, teal.

Alternative yarns: any DK to light worsted or Aran-weight yarn will substitute. If you cannot find a suitable metallic but want a sparkle, try holding your yarn with a strand of lurex to give subtle sheen.

MEASUREMENTS

Bust

81–86	91–97	102–107 cm
32–34	36–38	40–42 in

Actual Chest

97	108	120 cm
38¼	42½	47¼ in

Length from Shoulder

55	58	60 cm
21½	22¾	23½ in

TENSION/GAUGE

18 sts and 22 rows to 10 cm (4 in) in st st using 4.5 mm (US 7) knitting needles.

32 sts and 32 rows to 10 m (4 in) in 2x2 rib using 3.5 mm (US 4) needles.

NOTIONS

Pair of 3.5 mm (US 4) knitting needles
Pair of 4.5 mm (US 7) knitting needles
Stitch holders
Darning needle

SPECIAL INSTRUCTIONS

Fan Lace Panel (worked over 34 sts)

Row 1: *p1, k1tbl, k4tog, [yo, k1] 5 times, yo, k4tog, k1tbl, p1.
repeat from * once more.
Row 2: [k1, p15, k1] twice.
Row 3: [p1, k1tbl, k13, k1tbl, p1] twice.
Row 4: as row 2.

PATTERN

Back

**Using 3.5 mm (US 4) needles, cast on 98[106:118] sts and work 10 cm (4 in) in 2x2 rib as folls:
Row 1: k2, [p2, k2] to end of row.
Row 2: p2, [k2, p2] to end of row.
Ending with a row 2, decreasing 20[18:20] sts evenly along last row.
*78[88:98] sts***.

Change to 4.5 mm (US 7) needles and work straight in st st, increasing 1 st at either end of 5th and every foll 4th row until 88[98:108] sts.

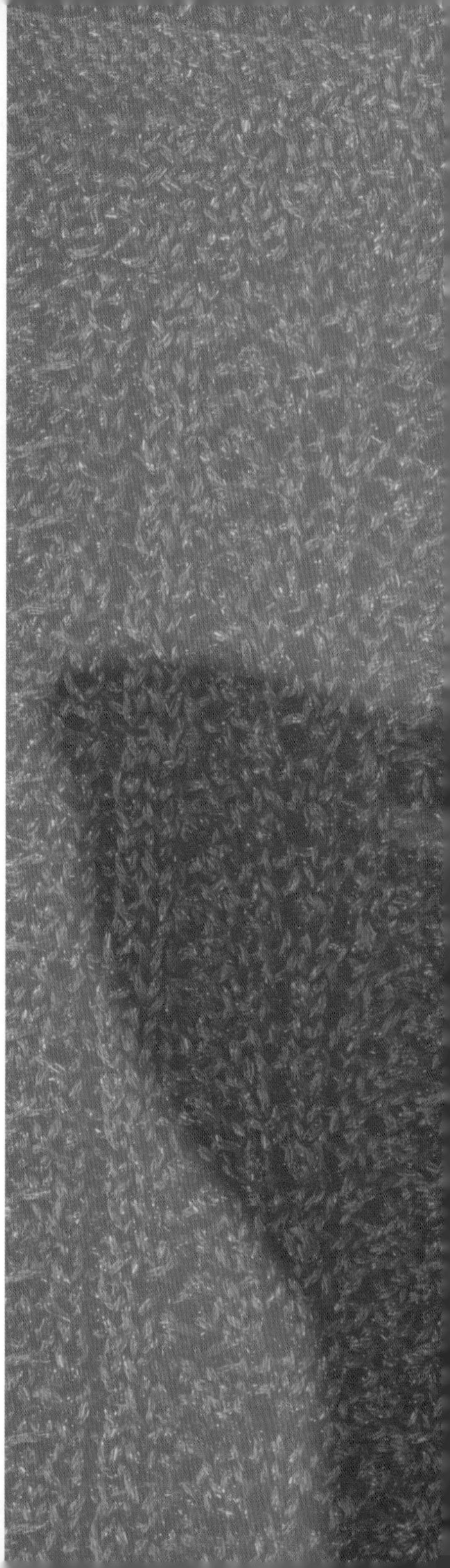

Far right: A sweater made in a glitzy metallic yarn can easily be dressed up for evening. Wear it with some skinny jeans and skyscraper heels for a night on the town or some tailored wide-legged trousers and wedges for dinner out.

Above: The deep ribbing at the waist serves to emphasize the oversized batwing and make the piece all that much more dramatic.

Above right: A long and lean ribbed sleeve cuts out a lot of the excess fabric that was typical of 1980s batwing sweaters and allows the fabric to puff out suddenly from the top of the cuff.

Cont straight on these sts in st st until work measures 14 cm (5½ in) from beg of st st, ending with a p row.

Cast on 4 sts at beg of every foll row until there are 168[178:188] sts, then cast on 2 sts at beg of every foll row until there are 188[198:208] sts.

Work straight until the piece measures 55[58:60] cm (21½ [22¾:23½] in), ending with a p row.
Next row: k76[80:84], place these sts on stitch holder, cast off 36[38:40] sts, k to end, placing these sts onto a second st holder.

Front

Work as for back between ** and **.
Change to 4.5 mm (US 7) needles and work as folls, increasing 1 st at either end of 5th and every foll 4th row until 88[98:108] sts:
Row 1: k22[27:32], PM work lace patt across next 34 sts, PM, k to end.
Row 2: p to marker, work lace patt across next 34 sts, p to end.
Row 3: k to marker, work lace patt across next 34 sts, k to end.
Rep rows 2 and 3 for front, increasing at either end as set.
Cont straight on these sts in patt until work measures 14 cm (5½ in) from beg of st st, ending with a WSR.

Cast on 4 sts at beg of every foll row until there are 168[178:188] sts, then cast on 2 sts at beg of every foll row until there are 188[198:208] sts.

Work straight until piece measures 49[52:54] cm (19¼ [20½:21¼] in), ending with a p row.

Next row: Patt over 88[92:96] sts, cast off 12[14:16], patt to end of row.

Work for right neck as folls:
Row 1: dec 1 st at end of row.
Row 2: cast off 3 sts, patt to end of row.
Cont for neck, dec 1 st at neck edge of every row until 76[80:84] sts rem.
Cont straight until work measures 55[58:60] cm (21½[22¾:23½] in) ending with a WSR.
Leave these sts on a holder and rejoin yarn to left neck edge.
Complete to match right neck.

Join right shoulder seam by grafting stitches together.

Neck Edging

Using 3.5 mm (US 4) needles, and with RSF, pick up and k17 sts down left side of neck, 12[14:16] sts across front neck cast-off sts, 17 sts up right front neck and 36[38:40] sts across cast-off sts at back neck. *82[86:90] sts.*
Work in 1x1 rib for 5 rows.

Change to 4.5 mm (US 7) needles and cont in 1x1 rib for a further 3 rows.

Cast off *very loosely* in rib.

Join rem shoulder seam by grafting.

Attach yarn to the bottom of the sleeve for cuff with 3.5 mm (US 4) needles and RSF and pick up and k 58[66:70] sts across edge. Work in 2x2 rib as for main body, beg with a row 2 and work straight until cuff measures 22[24:26] cm (8½[9½:10¼] in).
Rep for rem cuff.

Sew up underarm seams.

Left: A lace-panelled front adds interest to the expanse of fabric. When working the panel, be careful to ensure it is centred.

Striped Mohair Sweater

Fluffy mohair was used ubiquitously in sweaters, which were invariably oversized, brightly coloured and even embellished with beading or satin appliqué for evening. To bring this 1980s idea bang up to date, the sweater takes inspiration from the punk movement of the late 1970s and early 1980s, using the mohair on larger needles to create an open fabric and striping in two bold shades. The construction uses a drop shoulder sleeve, as many vintage patterns from this decade did, but with slightly tighter-fitting sleeves to avoid a lot of the volume that the traditional sweaters had. The mohair used here is also less fuzzy, which again avoids unnecessary bulk and also enhances the openness of the fabric.

YARNS

3(4:5) x 25 g (1 oz) balls of Rowan Kidsilk Haze, 70% mohair, 30% silk, 210 m (229 yds) in shade 641, blackcurrant (yarn A).

3(3:4) x 25 g (1 oz) balls of Rowan Kidsilk Haze, 70% mohair, 30% silk, 210 m (229 yds) in shade 606, candy girl (yarn B).

Alternative yarns: Any lightweight mohair will do here to create the soft, delicate and ethereal quality to the fabric. Alternatively, work the sweater in a heavier yarn such as a DK weight wool to create a dense sweater.

Left: A punk-style jumper need not be grungy. Team this cosy top with drainpipe trousers for a casual, easy style or even pair with leggings to wear as a daring sweater dress.

Right: The use of stripes in varying thicknesses creates an arresting contrast. The arms, however, could be knit in the same width as the body stripes or even in a solid colour for an alternative look.

MEASUREMENTS

Bust		
81–86	91–97	102–107 cm
32–34	36–38	40–42 in
Actual Size		
102	111	120 cm
40	43¾	47 in
Length from Shoulder		
60	62	64 cm
23½	24½	25 in
Sleeve Seam		
54	55	56 cm
21¼	21½	22 in
Armhole		
19	21	23 cm
7½	8¼	9 in

TENSION/GAUGE

18 sts and 22 rows to 10 cm (4 in) in st st using 5.5 mm (US 9) knitting needles.

20 sts and 28 rows to 10 cm (4 in) in st st using 4.5 mm (US 7) knitting needles.

NOTIONS

Pair of 3.75 mm (US 5) knitting needles

Pair of 4.5 mm (US 7) knitting needles

Pair of 5.5 mm (US 9) knitting needles

Darning needle

Below: The body is knit to a slightly looser tension than the arms, creating an ethereal fabric with a beautifully light and airy handle. You may find it harder to knit the yarn to a looser tension so take it slowly and try metal needles to ensure the smooth flow of the yarn over the needles.

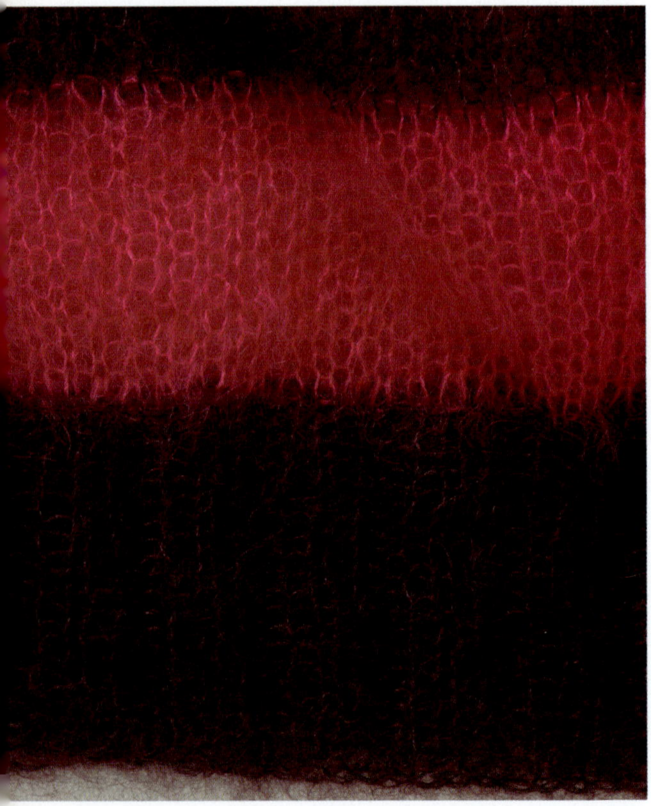

PATTERN

Back

Using 4.5 mm (US 7) knitting needles and yarn A, cast on 82[90:98] sts and work in 2x2 rib as folls:
Row 1: k2, *p2, k2; rep from * across row.
Row 2: p2, *k2, p2; rep from * across row.

Work 6 cm (2½ in) in rib as established, ending with a row 2.

Change to yarn B and 5.5 mm (US 9) needles and cont in st st, inc 1 st at either end of 13th and every foll 24th row until 92[100:108] sts, working in 6 cm (2½ in) stripes of yarn B and A alternately.

Cont straight in st st, striping as established, until work measures 60[62:64] cm (23½[24½:25] in) from cast-on edge, ending with a p row.

Shape Shoulders

Cast off 7[7:8]sts at beg of next 2 rows, then 6[8:9] sts at beg of foll 4 rows. Leave rem 54[54:56]sts on holder for back neck.

Front

Work as for back until piece measures 56 [58:60] cm (22[23:23½] in) from cast-on edge, ending with a p row.

Shape Front Neck

Next row: k30[34:37], cast off next 32[32:34] sts, k to end.

Work on 30[34:37]sts for right neck as folls:
Next row: p to last 2 sts, p2tog.
29[33:36] sts.
Next row: cast off 3 sts, k to end.
26[30:33] sts.
Rep last 2 rows once more.
22[26:29] sts.

Cont in st st, dec 1 st at neck edge of every foll row until 19[23:26] sts rem. Work straight on these sts, if necessary, until right front measures the same as back-to-shoulder shaping, ending with a k row.

Cast off 7[7:8] sts at beg of next row, then 6[8:9] sts at beg of foll 2 alt rows.

Rejoin yarn to neck edge of left front and complete to match right front, reversing shapings.

Sleeves

Using 3.75 mm (US 5) needles and yarn A, cast on 46[50:54] sts and work in 2x2 rib as folls:
Row 1: k2, *p2, k2; rep from * across row.
Row 2: p2, *k2, p2; rep from * across row.
Work 18 cm (7 in) in rib as established, ending with a row 2.

Change to yarn B and 4.5 mm (US 7) needles and cont in st st.

Two smallest sizes only:
Inc 1 st at either end of next row.

All sizes:
Inc 1 st at either end of every foll 7th[6th:5th] row until 76[84:92] sts, working 4 row stripes of yarn B and A alternately.

Cont straight in st st, striping as established, until work measures 54[55:56] cm (21¼[21½:22] in) from cast-on edge, ending with a p row.

Cast off all sts loosely.

Block all pieces very lightly to shape.

Neckband

Join right shoulder seam using a fine backstitch.

With RSF and using 3.75 mm (US 5) needles and yarn A, pick up and k26 sts down left front shaping, k32[32:34] sts from cast off at front neck, k26 sts up right front shaping. k across 54[54:56] sts left on holder at back of neck. *138[138:142] sts.*

Beg with row 2 of 2x2 rib pattern work in rib for 8 rows.

Cast off loosely in rib using a 4.5 mm (US 7) needle.

Finishing

Join rem shoulder seam.

Attach sleeves to body. To mark position, fold sleeves in half and PM at the fold at the top of the sleeve. Match this marker to the shoulder seam and sew evenly to body.

Sew up side and sleeve seams.

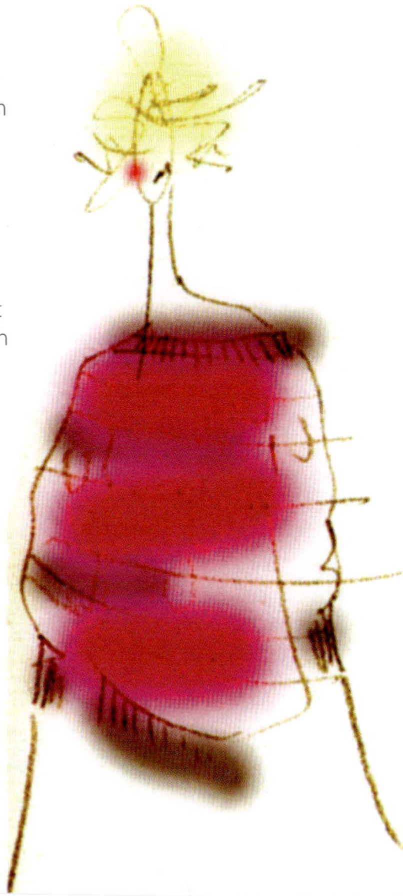

Cropped Cable-Knit Sweater

Cropped sweaters were high fashion in this decade, both from the areas of casual sportswear – showing off the newly aerobicized midriff – and from a modernist, fashion perspective with boxy shapes worn layered over baggy shirts, tops and trousers. Often paired with jeans and low-slung belts, the cropped top appeared in both a sleeveless version and one with extra-long sleeves. This cable-knit adaptation is made to be worn layered over slightly fitted clothing or even over a maxi jersey dress.

YARN

7(8:10:11) x 50 g (2 oz) balls of Punte del Este Mericash, 80% merino, 20% mongolian cashmere, 240 m (262 yds) in shade 321.

MEASUREMENTS

Actual Bust

77	82.5	92	101.5 cm
30½	32½	36¼	40 in

Length from Shoulder

33	35	37.5	40.5 cm
13	13¾	14¾	15¾ in

Sleeve Seam

49	51	52	54 cm
19¼	20	20½	21¼ in

NOTE: This is modelled with approx 3 cm (1¼ in) of positive ease.

TENSION/GAUGE

22 sts and 30 rows to 10 cm (4 in) in st st using 4 mm (US 6) knitting needles, or size required to obtain gauge and with yarn held double.

32 sts and 40 rows to 10 cm (4 in) in st st using 3.5 mm (US 4) knitting needles, or size required to obtain gauge with one strand of yarn.

NOTIONS

Pair of 2.5 mm (US 1½) knitting needles

Pair of 4 mm (US 6) knitting needles

Cable needle

Stitch holders

Darning needle

SPECIAL INSTRUCTIONS

C4F = Cable 4 forward: place next 2 sts on cn at front of work, knitting foll 2 sts from LHN, then knitting 2 sts from cn.

C4B = Cable 4 back: place next 2 sts on cn at back of work, knitting foll 2 sts from LHN, then knitting 2 sts from cn.

C8F = Cable 8 forward: place next 4 sts on cn at front of work, knitting foll 4 sts from LHN, then knitting 4 sts from cn.

C8B = Cable 8 back: place next 4 sts on cn at back of work, knitting foll 4 sts from LHN, then knitting 4 sts from cn.

NOTE: See also chart, page 156, for cable panels.

Right: This unusual length of sweater would also look fabulous over a figure-hugging jersey maxi dress or a simple black vest and jeans. Try to keep the styling classic, unless you really are going for a full retro look.

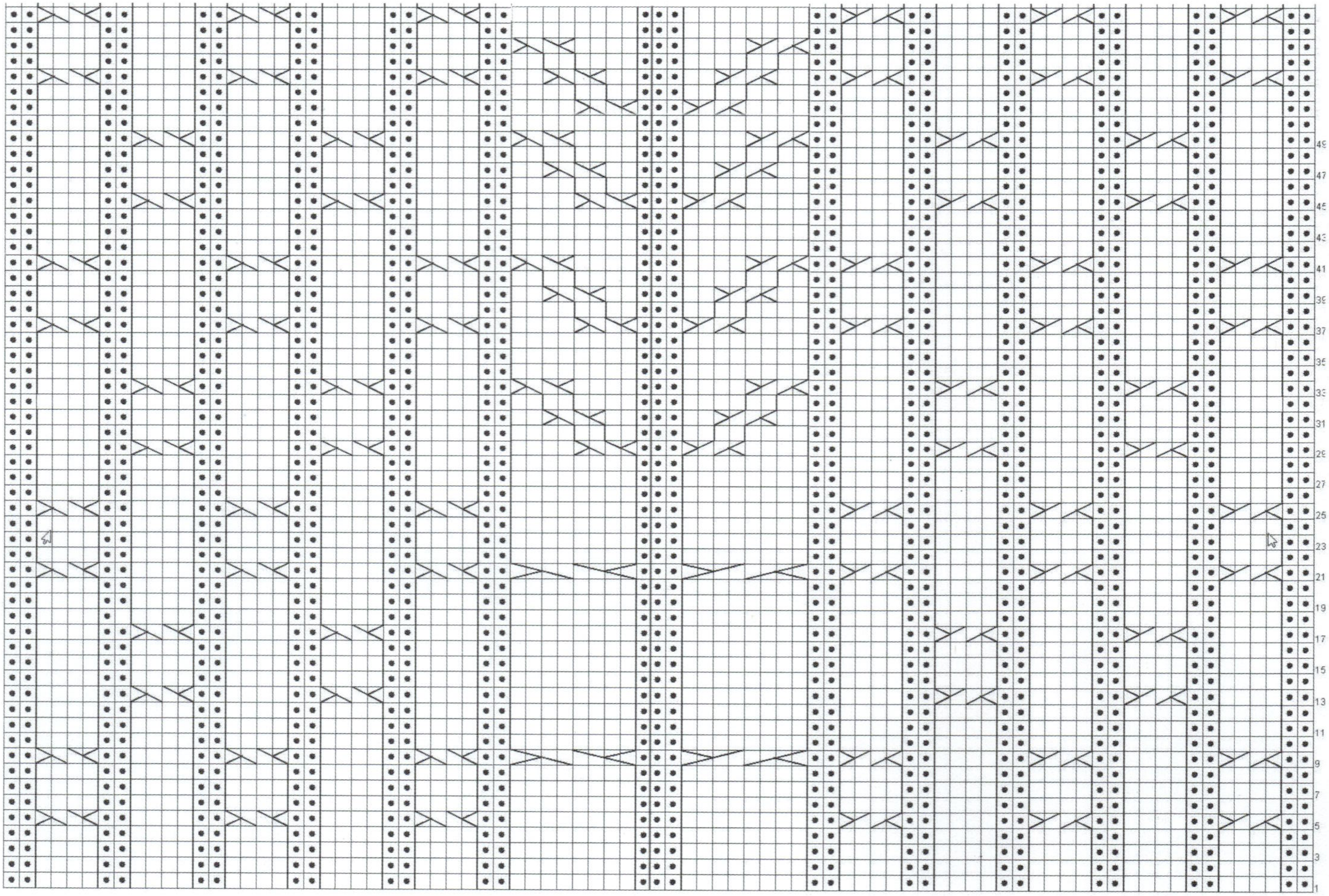

Key

Knit on RSR; Purl on a WSR

Purl on a RSR; Knit on a WSR

C4B

C4F

C8F

C8B

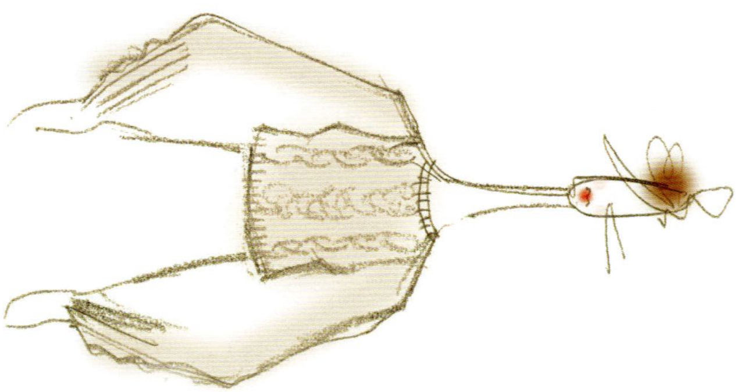

Left: Working the cables as a reflection through the centre panel creates an attractive patterning across the front of the sweater.

Cable Panel 1
(5 small cables worked over 30 sts)
Row 1(RS): [p2, k4] 5 times.
Row 2 (and every even/WS row): [p4, k2] 5 times.
These two rows form panel rib patt.
Rep last 2 rows once more.
Row 5: [p2, C4B, p2, k4] twice, p2, C4B.
Work 3 rows in panel rib patt, beg with row 2.
Row 9: as row 5.
Work 3 rows in panel rib patt, beg with row 2.
Row 13: [p2, k4, p2, C4B] twice, p2, k4.
Work 3 rows in panel rib patt, beg with row 2.
Row 17: as row 13.
Work 3 rows in panel rib patt, beg with row 2.
Rep rows 5 to 20 throughout for panel 1.

Cable Panel 2
(2 wide cables worked over 19 sts)
Inc 4 sts in row 1 to balance cable patt.
Row 1(RS): k2, m1, k2, m1, k2, p3, k2, m1, k2, m1, k2. *19 sts.*
Row 2 (and every even/WSR): p8, k3, p8.
Row 3: k8, p3, k8.
Rows 2 and 3 form panel rib patt.
Rep these 2 further times, then row 2 once more.
Row 9: C8B, p3, C8F
Work 11 rows in panel rib patt.
Row 21: as row 9.
Work 7 rows in panel rib patt.
Row 29: k4, C4B, p3, C4F, k4.
Row 31: k2, C4B, k2, p3, k2, C4F, k2.
Row 33: C4B, k4, p3, k4, C4F.
Work 3 rows in panel rib patt.
Rep rows 29 to 36 once more.
Row 45: k4, C4B, p3, C4F, k4.
Row 47: k2, C4B, k2, p3, k2, C4F, k2.
Row 49: C4B, k4, p3, k4, C4F.
Row 50: p8, k3, p8.
Rep rows 45 to 50 throughout for rem of panel 2.

Cable Panel 3
(5 small cables worked over 30 sts)
Row 1(RS): [k4, p2] 5 times.
Row 2 (and every even/WSR): [k2, p4] 5 times.
These 2 rows form panel rib patt.
Rep last 2 rows once more.
Row 5: [C4F, p2, k4, p2] twice, C4F, p2.
Work 3 rows in panel rib patt, beg with row 2.
Row 9: as row 5

Right: A crewneck is a simple shape that is used effectively here to cut across the cable patterning without detracting from it.

Work 3 rows in panel rib patt, beg with row 2.
Row 13: [k4, p2, C4F, p2] twice, k4, p2.
Work 3 rows in panel rib patt, beg with row 2.
Row 17: as row 13.
Work 3 rows in panel rib patt, beg with row 2.
Rep rows 5 to 20 throughout for panel 3.

PATTERN
Back
Using 4 mm (US 6) knitting needles and the yarn held double, cast on 85[91:101:113] sts.
Row 1(RS): k1, *p1, k1, rep from * to end of row.
Row 2: p1, *k1, p1, rep from * to end of row.
These 2 rows form patt. Rep until rib measures 2 cm (¾ in) from cast-on edge, ending with a row 2.

Beg with a k row, work straight in st st until work measures 16[17:18:20] cm (6¼[6¾:7:7¾] in) from cast-on edge, or desired length to underarm, ending with a WSR.

Shape Armholes
Cast off 5[5:6:7] sts at beg of next 2 rows. *75[81:89:99] sts.*
Now dec 1 st at either end of every row 3[3:5:5] times, then each end of every RS row 0[0:0:2] times.
69[75:79:85] sts.

Work straight until armhole measures 17[18:19.5:20.5] cm (6¾[7:7¾:8] in) from beg of shaping ending with a WSR.

Shape Shoulders
Cast off 5[5:6:7] sts at beg of 4 foll rows and 5[6:6:6] sts at beg of next 2 rows.
Leave rem 39[43:43:45] sts on holder for back neck.

Front
Using 4 mm (US 6) needles and the yarn held double, cast on 89[95:105:117] sts.
Row 1(RS): k1, *p1, k1, rep from * to end of row.
Row 2: p1, *k1, p1, rep from * to end of row.
These 2 rows form pattern. Rep until rib measures 2 cm (¾ in) from cast-on edge, ending with a row 2.

Beginning all panels at first row, work cable pattern as folls (alternatively, follow chart):
Row 1(RS): k5[8:13:19], panel one1 p2, panel 2, p2, panel 3, k5[8:13:19].
93[99:109:121] sts.
Row 2: p5[8:13:19], panel 3, k2, panel 2, k2, panel 1, p5[8:13:19].
Last 2 rows form cable patt, cont in this way until work measures the same as the back-to-armholes measurement.

Shape Armholes
Cont in patt, cast off 5[5:6:7] sts at beg of next 2 rows. *83[89:97:107] sts.*

Now dec one st at either end of every row 3[3:5:5] times, then each end of every RSR 0[0:0:2] times.
77[83:87:93] sts.

Work straight in cable patt until armhole measures 12[12.5:13.5:14] cm (4¾[5:5¼:5½] in) from beg of armhole shaping, ending with a WSR.

Shape Neck

Patt across 27[30:32:35] sts, then cast off next 23 sts, treating the 8 st cables as 6 st cables by working k2tog twice evenly across each cable while casting off, patt to end of row.

Turn and work on these 27[30:32:35] sts for right neck in established cable patt as folls:

Cast off 3 sts at neck edge of foll RSR, cont in patt to end of row. *24[27:29:32] sts.*

Then dec one st at neck edge on every foll row until 15[16:18:20] sts rem.

Work straight on these sts until work measures the same as the back-to-shoulder shaping, ending with a RSR.

Shape Shoulder

Cast off 5[5:6:7] sts at beg of 2 foll WSRs and 5[6:6:6] sts at beg of next WSR.

Left Neck

Rejoin yarn to WS of left neck edge, and cont on these 27[30:32:35] sts as folls: Cast off 3 sts at beg of next row, cont in patt to end of row. *24[27:29:32] sts.*

Now dec one st at neck edge on every foll row until 15[16:18:20] sts rem.

Work straight on these sts until work measures the same as the back-to-shoulder shaping, ending with a WSR.

Shape Shoulder

Cast off 5[5:6:7] sts at beg of 2 foll RSRs and 5[6:6:6] sts at beg of next RSR.

Sleeves

Using 2.5 mm (US 1½) needles and a single strand of yarn, cast on 69[75:85:91] sts.

Row 1: k1, *p1, k1, rep from * to end of row.

Row 2: p1, *k1, p1, rep from * to end of row.

These two rows form patt, rep until rib measures 18 cm(7 in) from cast-on edge.

Change to st st and inc 1 st at either end of 19th[19th:19th:17th] and then every foll 20th[20th:18th:16th] row 5[5:6:7] times. *81[87:99:107] sts.*

Work straight until work measures 49[51:52:54] cm (19¼[20:20½:21¼] in) from cast-on edge, ending with a WSR.

Shape Sleeve Top

Cont in st st, cast off 5[5:6:7] sts at beg of next two rows. *71[77:87:93] sts.*

Now dec 1 st at either end of every row 3[3:5:7] times, then each end of every RSR 5[6:5:4] times. *55[59:67:71] sts.*

Dec 1 st at either end of every foll 4th row 5[5:6:5] times, then at either end of every following RSR 4[5:6:8] times, at either end of every foll row 5[5:5:5] times, then cast off 3[3:4:4] sts at beg of next 4 rows, cast off rem 15[17:17:19] sts.

Finishing

Block all pieces lightly.
Join right shoulder seam using mattress stitch.

Using 4 mm (US 6) needles and the yarn held double, rejoin yarn to front left neck, pick up and k evenly 11[12:13:14] sts down left neck, 19 sts along centre-front neck, 11[12:13:14] sts up right neck, then k along 39[43:43:45] sts on holder for back neck. *80[86:88:92] sts.*

Turn and work 4 rows 1x1 rib on these sts, cast off all sts loosely.
Join rem shoulder and neck seam.

Set in sleeves using mattress st, then sew underarm and side seams using mattress st.

Above: Fully-fashioned edging creates a tidy seam; follow the line of the shaping when sewing up to ensure your join remains neat.

Neon Fingerless Gloves

Pop stars such as Madonna made short lacy gloves fashionable in the 1980s. This warmer, more practical version is great if you want to keep your hands warm but still need full use of your fingers – always good when working, shopping or socializing outdoors in the winter.

YARN

1 x 50 g (2 oz) ball of BC Garn Silkbloom, 55% merino, 45% mulberry silk, 140 m (153 yds) in shade 18, blood orange.

Alternative yarns: any light Aran or worsted weight yarn.

MEASUREMENTS

One size.

TENSION/GAUGE

20 sts and 28 rows to 10 cm (4 in) in st st using 4.5 mm (US 7) double pointed knitting needles.

NOTIONS

Set of 3.5 mm (US 4) double pointed needles
Set of 4.5 mm (US 7) double pointed needles
Stitch markers
Cable needle
Darning needle

SPECIAL INSTRUCTIONS

RC3 = Right Cable 3: slip next 2 sts onto cn and hold at back of work, k next st from LHN, then k 2 sts from cn.

LC3 = Left Cable 3: slip next st onto cn and hold at front of work, k next 2 sts from LHN, then k st from cn.

Cable Panel (worked over 9 sts)

Start from row 1.
Rnd 1 to 3: p1, k7, p1.
Rnd 4: p1, RC3, k1, LC3, p1.
These 4 rnds form pattern, rep for panel.

Far left: The cropped shape of these gloves looks great when worn with bracelet-length sleeves to make a fashion statement – as opposed to keeping your hands warm!

Left: A fishbone cable is a very pretty technique and a no-nonsense way to decorate fingerless gloves

PATTERN

Right Glove

Using 3.5 mm (US 4) dpns cast on 40 sts and arrange for working in the rnd.
Work 2 cm (¾ in) in 1x1 rib on these sts.

Change to 4.5 mm (US 7) dpns and work as folls:
Rnd 1 to 5: k5, cable panel, k to end of rnd.
Rnd 6: k5, cable panel, k5, m1, k1, PM, m1, k to end of rnd.
Rnd 7: patt across, knitting over increased sts.
Rnd 8: patt to st before marker, m1, k1, sl marker, m1 patt to end.
Work these last 2 rnds until there are 50 sts.

Next row: patt 30, turn, leaving rem sts unworked.

Cast on 2 sts at beg of next row, k11 sts, turn, leaving rem sts unworked.

Cast on1 sts at beg of next row.
**Work on these 14 for 2 cm (¾ in), then work 3 rows 1x1 rib.

Cast off all sts loosely.

Rejoin yarn to unworked sts, inc 1 and work to end of rnd. *40 sts.*

Resume working in rnd.

Next rnd: patt to end.
Cont in pattern on these 40 sts for a further 2.5 cm (1 in).

Work 2 cm (¾ in) in 1x1 rib.

Cast off all sts loosely.

Sew up thumb seam and gap at bottom of thumb.

Weave in all ends and block lightly.

Left Glove

Using 3.5 mm (US 4) dpns, cast on 40 sts and arrange for working in the rnd.

Work 2 cm (¾ in) in 1 x 1rib on these sts.

Change to 4.5 mm (US 7) dpns and work as folls:
Rnd 1 to 5: k26, cable panel, k to end of rnd.
Rnd 6: k20, m1, k1, PM, m1, cable panel, k to end of rnd.
Rnd 7: patt across, knitting over increased sts.
Rnd 8: patt to st before marker, m1, k1, sl marker, m1 patt to end.
Work these last 2 rnds until there are 50 sts.

Next row: patt 31, turn, leaving rem sts unworked.

Cast on 2 sts at beg of next row, k11 sts, turn, leaving rem sts unworked.

Cast on 1 sts at beg of next row.
Finish as for right glove from **.

Fun Navy Legwarmers

As sportswear began to merge with streetwear in the 1980s, the aerobics and fitness craze saw leggings, leotards and legwarmers hit the high street and become popular for the everyday, rather than being reserved strictly for the gym or dance studio. Today, this simple and classic pattern creates a warm ankle cosy that can be worn while relaxing around the house or as a fashion statement over jeans and heels on a very cold day. They also look great worn with wellies, peeking over the top of the boot, paired with a skirt, providing extra warmth for outdoor walks or activities. You can knit them as long or as short as you like; due to the stretchiness of the rib, they will adapt to the contours of your leg.

YARN
2 x 100g (4 oz) balls of Artesano Aran 50% alpaca, 50% wool, 132 m (144 yds) in shade C834.

Alternative yarns: any Aran or worsted weight yarn with a light and fluffy handle will make these warmers extra cosy!

MEASUREMENTS
To fit S[M:L] adult leg.
Width (unstretched) is 23[25:27] cm (9[9¾:10½] in) in circumference.
Length (unstretched) is 52 cm (20½ in).

TENSION/GAUGE
22 sts and 24 rows to 10 cm (4 in) in st st using 5 mm (US 8) knitting needles.

NOTIONS
Set of 5 mm (US 8) double-pointed needles
Darning needle

PATTERN
Using 5 mm (US 8) dpn, cast on 52[56:60] sts using the longtail method and join for working in the round, PM to mark beg of rnd.

Rnd 1: [k1, p1] to end of rnd.
Rep rnd 1 for approx 52 cm (20½ in), or to desired length.

Cast off all sts very loosely so that the warmers can fit over all the widest contours of the leg.

Below: The chunky all-over ribbing allows the fabric to stretch and contract over the contours of the leg, so that no shaping is required. Because they are not fitted as such, you can make them as long or short as you wish.

Right: Only pair these legwarmers with a leotard if you are going to dance class or recreating a retro 1980s look. A modern way to style them is over skinny jeans or under wellies.

Resources

Vintage Haberdashers & Stockists

UK

Alfie's Antique Market
13–25 Church Street
London NW8 8DT
Tel: 020 7723 6066
www.alfiesantiques.com

Alfie's Antique Market has stalls for vintage fabrics, fashion and accessories. The dealers include: Deborah Woolf, Empire Vintage, Hell to Pay, Zoe Lloyd, June Victor, Nigel Martina and Persiflage. There is also a café on the rooftop of the market building.

The Button Queen
76 Marylebone Lane
London W1U 2PR
Tel: 020 7935 1505
www.thebuttonqueen.co.uk

The Button Queen specializes in button coverings and the sale of individual buttons. They stock a range of styles such as Art Nouveau silver and Art Deco plastics. They also stock menswear buttons, from dress shirt studs to dinner jacket buttons.

Deborah Woolf
28 Church Street
London NW8 8EP
www.deborahwoolf.com

Deborah Woolf stocks a variety of clothing and fabrics, from antique folk costume to avant-garde clothing. There is a range of items dating from the 1920s up until the 1980s, including famous brands such as Givenchy, Gucci and 1970s Laura Ashley. They have even loaned some of their items to TV and film productions and the V&A for their exhibition *The Golden Age of Couture, Paris and London 1947–57*.

Donna Flower
Lendon House
Abbotsham, Bideford
Devon EX39 5BW
Tel: 0845 4735095
www.donnaflower.com

Donna Flower sell unique and one-off antique fabrics from the nineteenth century to fabrics from the 1940s, 1950s, 1960s, 1970s and 1980s. They scour French flea markets to find these distinctive and interesting fabrics, which are perfect for creating a vintage outfit.

Fur Coat No Knickers
Top Floor
Kingly Court
Carnaby Street
London W1B 5PW
Tel: 07814 002 295
www.furcoatnoknickers.co.uk

Fur Coat No Knickers is a dressmaker's and has a shop on Carnaby Street, London, where they make made-to-measure wedding dresses using vintage patterns. There are also vintage wedding dresses, already made, which can be altered to fit. They also sell vintage accessories.

Louise Loves
Vintage Mercantile
1 Back Fold
Hay-on-Wye
HR3 5EQ
Tel: 01497 820 415
www.louiseloves.co.uk

Louise Loves sells vintage-style fabrics, which are especially designed to compliment vintage pieces, and vintage products; the vintage depot stocks a range of items from eiderdowns to teacups. They also sell patchwork and craft pieces, and have a shop in Hay-on-Wye called Bricks and Mortar.

Nichols Buttons
Tel: 020 7701 3433
www.nicholsbuttons.co.uk

Lionel Nichols makes and sells his own buttons. He worked alone as a glassmaker, and from 1946 to 1966 he handmade the couture buttons seen on this website today. Dixie Nichols, his daughter, is gradually selling the remaining buttons. There are four selections of buttons offered each year; they sell out fast and prices rise quite steeply each time the buttons are put up for sale. To be notified as to when the buttons will be up for sale, it is best to join the newsletter, which can be done so through the website.

Rag Rescue
Tel: 07848 761 470
www.ragrescue.co.uk

Rag Rescue is a company that recovers vintage fabrics and trims and then cleans them for re-use to sell through the website. New items are listed every day of the week and include vintage fabric squares, vintage buttons and vintage lace. The website is organized into colours, sizes, florals, checks and stripes, and so on, making it easy to find exactly what you are looking for.

Spinster's Emporium
www.spinstersemporium.co.uk

Spinster's Emporium's aim is to find pieces that complement knitwear; all the stock is limited or vintage. Each fabric or haberdashery item is handpicked and bought specifically for its design, quality and uniqueness. The website stocks vintage fabric, knitting yarn, haberdashery, vintage buttons, vintage patterns and vintage wallpaper. They also run workshops in Brighton, Cambridge, London and Nottingham.

VV Rouleaux
Sloane Square
261 Pavilion Road
Sloane Square
London SW1X 0PB
Tel: 020 7730 3125

102 Marylebone Lane
Marylebone
London W1U 2QD
Tel: 020 7224 5179
www.vvrouleaux.com

VV Rouleaux is a well-known brand specializing in ribbons, trimmings, tassels, tie-backs, flowers, display and Christmas decorations, as well as interior and fashion accessories. It is the perfect place to find decoration or detailing to add to your knitwear.

USA

Accessories of Old
151 North Market Street
Frederick, MD 21701
Tel: 301 760 7228
www.accessoriesofold.com

Accessories of Old sell vintage buttons from novelty plastic to antique glass. Pins, ribbons, sequins, buckles and brooches are also available.

Artbeads
11901 137th Avenue Ct. KPM
Gig Harbor, WA 98329
Tel: 1 866 715 BEAD
www.artbeads.com

A great resource for all types of beads, sequins and Swarovski crystals, as well as jewellery findings.

Contemporary Cloth
P O Box 733
Willoughby, OH 44094-0733
Tel: 866 415 3372
www.contemporarycloth.com

Contemporary Cloth stocks modern, hand-dyed and vintage fabrics, including novelty fabrics. They also sell patterns and stencils.

DeWitt & Co
PO Box 234
De Witt, NE 68341-0234
Tel: 402 683 2515
http://dewittco.com/VintageFabric

The website sells many vintage fabrics and patterns as well as other vintage clothing and household items.

GB Buttons
www.gbbuttons.com

This website stocks a range of vintage buttons with new arrivals coming in frequently. They carry antique Bakelite, glass, wood, ceramic, uniform buttons and many more.

Material Pleasures, LLC
Dana Balsamo
41 Taylor Road
Princeton NJ 08540
Tel: 732 221 3560
www.materialpleasures.com

This website sells vintage haberdashery and buttons, as well as sewing patterns from the 1940s. It also has a large stock of Victorian clothing.

Sharon's Antiques Vintage Fabrics
Tel: 610 756 6048
www.rickrack.com

This website sells a range of vintage fabrics from the 1920s to the 1960s. To help you size the designs, there is a coin placed on each piece of fabric to give you an idea of proportion. All fabrics are cotton unless otherwise stated.

Urban Burp
170 Columbus Ave, Suite 110
San Francisco CA 94133
Tel: 415 399 8761
www.urbanburp.com

Urban Burp sell rare vintage fabrics from tropical styles to upholstery material as well as novelty fabrics. They also stock reproduction fabrics using similar patterns to the vintage fabric they stock.

Vintage Knitting Patterns

Skiff Vintage Knitting Patterns
10–11 Timberyard Cottages
Lewes, East Sussex BN7 2AX
www.skiffvintageknittingpatterns.co.uk

This website is divided into brands, eras and garments. They stock patterns by brands such as Bairns-Wear and Robin. The patterns range in decades from the 1930s to the 1960s.

Victoria & Albert Museum, London
Cromwell Road
London SW7 2RL
Tel: 020 7942 2000
www.vam.ac.uk/collections/fashion/features/knitting/1940s/index.html

The Archive of Art and Design at the V&A holds a small collection of knitting patterns including wartime knitting and general knitting. All the designs are free to download.

The Vintage Knitting Lady
64 Masefield Road
Warminster BA12 8HY
Tel: 01980 625486
www.theretroknittingcompany.co.uk
www.thevintageknittinglady.co.uk

The collection of vintage knitting patterns from the 1920s to the 1970s includes baby's and doll's clothes as well as men, women and children's fashions. They also carry vintage yarns, buttons, needles and accessories.

Vintage Knitted Couture
69 Hampton Park
Bristol BS6 6LQ GB
Tel: 0117 377 5608
www.vintageknittedcouture.com

Patterns are available for both crochet and knitting and include a wide range of projects, from dresses and shrugs to baby clothes and cushions.

Yesterknits
33 Hillside Crescent
Edinburgh EH7 5EF
Scotland
Tel: 0131 556 3436
www.yesterknits.com

Yesterknits has the largest collection of vintage knitting and crochet patterns in the world. They are based in Scotland and stock patterns from 1880–1980. There is even the option to get a selection of 16 free patterns via email through the website.

Knitting Shops & Emporiums

UK

All the Fun of the Fair
Unit 2.8 Kingly Court
Carnaby Street
London W1B 5PW
Tel: 07905 075017
www.allthefunofthefair.biz

Artyarn
10 High Street
Pointon, Sleaford
Lincolnshire NG34 0LX
Tel: 01529 240510
www.artyarn.co.uk (online only)

Bicester Wools
Rowland & Ellie Hewison
19 Deans Court
Bicester
Oxon
OX26 6RD
www.bicesterwools.com/

Coats Crafts UK
Green Lane Mill
Holmfirth
West Yorkshire HD9 2DX
Tel: 01484 681881
www.coatscrafts.co.uk (online only)

Get Knitted
39 Brislington Hill
Brislington
Bristol
BS4 5BE
www.getknitted.com/

I Knit London
106 Lower Marsh
Waterloo, London SE1 7AB
Tel: 020 7261 1338
www.iknit.org.uk

K1 Knitting Boutique
136 Queen Margaret Drive
Glasgow
G20 8NY

89 West Bow
Edinburgh
EH1 2JP
www.k1yarns.com/woolshop/

The Knitting Shop
79 Gillespie Road
Islington, London N5 1LR
Tel: 020 7226 0800
www.knittingwoolandyarnshop.co.uk

Loop Yarn Shop
15 Camden Passage
Islington
London N1 8EA
Tel: 020 7288 1160
www.loopknitting.com

Mrs Moon Yarn Haberdashery
41 Crown Road
St Margarets, Twickenham TW1 3EJ
Tel: 020 8744 1190
www.mrsmoon.co.uk

Nest
102 Weston Park
Crouch End, London N8 9PP
Tel: 020 8340 8852
www.handmadenest.co.uk

Patricia Roberts
60 Kinnerton Street
Belgravia, London SW1X 8ES
Tel: 020 7235 4742
www.patriciaroberts.co.uk

Sew-In of Marple and Didsbury
741 Wilmslow Road
Didsbury
Manchester
M20 6RN

46 Market Street
Marple
Cheshire
SK6 7AD
www.knitting-and-needlework.co.uk/

US

Classic Elite Yarns
122 Western Avenue
Lowell, MA 01851
Tel: 978 453 2837
www.classiceliteyarns.com (online only)

Halcyon Yarn
12 School Street
Bath, ME 04530
Tel: 800 341 0282
www.halcyonyarn.com

ImagiKnit
3897 18th Street
San Francisco, CA 94114
Tel: 415 621 6642
www.imagiknit.com

Kaleidoscope Yarns
15 Pearl Street
Essex Junction, VT 05452
Tel: 802 288 9200
www.kyarns.com (online only)

Purl Soho
459 Broome Street
New York, NY 10013
Tel: 212 420 8796
www.purlsoho.com

Sophie's Yarns
739 South 4th Street
Philadelphia, PA 19147
Tel: 215 825 KNIT
www.sophiesyarns.com

CANADA

Knit & Purl
10412 124th Street
Edmonton, Alberta
T5N 1R5
Tel: 780 482 2150

Magasin de Fibre Lb Inc.
2270 Mont-Royal East
Montreal, Québec H2H 1K6
Tel: 514 521 9000

Yarn Suppliers

UK

Artesano Ltd
Unit G, Lamb's Farm Business Park
Basingstoke Road
Swallowfield
Reading, Berkshire RG7 1PQ
Tel: 01189 503 350
www.artesanoyarns.co.uk

Designer Yarns, Ltd
Unit 8–10 Newbridge Industrial Estate
Pitt Street
Keighley, West Yorkshire BD21 4PQ
Tel: 01535 664222
www.designeryarns.uk.com

Fyberspates
The Maintenance Room
The Nalder Estate
East Challow, Nr Wantage
Oxfordshire OX12 9SY
Tel: 07540 656 660
www.fyberspates.co.uk

Jamieson's of Shetland
Sandness Industrial Estate
Sandness, Shetland ZE2 9PL
Scotland
Tel: 01595 870 285
www.jamiesonsshetland.co.uk

King Cole Ltd
Merrie Mills
Elliott Street
Silsden
Keighley,West Yorkshire BD20 0DE
Tel: 01535 650 230
www.kingcole.co.uk

Malabrigo Yarn
Tel: 020 3318 5173
europa@malabrigoyarn.com
www.malabrigoyarn.com

Orkney Angora
Isle of Sanday
Orkney, Scotland KW17 2AZ
Tel: 01857 600 421
www.orkneyangora.co.uk

Rowan
Tel: 01484 681 881
www.knitrowan.com

Shilasdair Skye Yarn Co
10 Carnach, Waternish
Isle of Skye, Scotland IV55 8GL
Tel: 01470 592 297
www.shilasdair-yarns.co.uk
www.theskyeshilasdairshop.co.uk

US

Berroco Inc
14 Elmdale Road
PO Box 367
Uxbridge, MA 01569
Tel: 508 278 2527
www.berroco.com

Blue Sky Alpacas Inc.
PO Box 88
Cedar, MN 55011
Tel: 763 753 5815/888 460 8862
www.blueskyalpacas.com

Brown Sheep Company, Inc.
100662 County Road 16
Mitchell NE 69357
Tel: 800 826 9135
www.brownsheep.com

Karabella Yarns Inc.
1201 Broadway
New York, NY 10001
Tel: 212 684 2665
www.karabellayarns.com

Knitting Fever
PO Box 336
315 Bayview Ave
Amityville, NY 11701
Tel: 516 546 3600
www.knittingfever.com

Knit One Crochet Too Yarn
91 Tandberg Trail
Unit 6
Windham, ME 04062
Tel: 207 892 9625
www.knitonecrochettoo.com

Koigu Wool Designs
PO Box 158
Chatsworth, ON N0H 1G0
Tel: 888 765 WOOL
www.koigu.com

Knitcellaneous
(Distributes Fyberspates)
120 Acorn Street
Merlin, OR 97532
Tel: 541 955 9348
www.knitcellaneous.com

Lion Brand Yarn
135 Kero Road
Carlstadt, NJ 07072
Tel: 1 800 661- 7551
www.lionbrand.com

Malabrigo Yarn
Tel: 786 866 6167
www.malabrigoyarn.com

Muench Yarns Inc.
(Distributes GGH)
1323 Scott Street
Petaluma, CA 94954-1135
Tel: 800 733 9276
www.muenchyarns.com

Tahki • Stacy Charles, Inc
70–30 80th Street
Building 36
Ridgewood, NY 11385
Tel: 800 338 YARN
www.tahkistacycharles.com

Trendsetter Yarns
16745 Saticoy Street Suite #101
Van Nuys, CA 91406
Tel: 818 780 5497
www.trendsetteryarns.com

Punta Yarns
Duchess Fibers
132 Church Street
PO Box 221
Millbrook, NY 12545
Tel: 845 677 4601
www.puntayarns.com

Unique Kolours
(Distributes Mission Falls)
28 North Bacton Hill Road
Malvern, PA 19335
Tel: 800 252 DYE4
www.uniquekoloursusa.com

Westminster Fibers Inc.
165 Ledge Street
Nashua, NH 03060
Tel: 800 445 9276
www.westminsterfibers.com

CANADA

Diamond Yarn
155 Martin Ross Avenue
Unit 3
Toronto, Ontario M3J 2L9

9697 Boulevard St. Laurent,
Porte 101
Montréal, Québec H3L 2N1
www.diamondyarn.com

Estelle Design and Sales Limited
2220 Midland Avenue
Unit 65
Scarborough, Ontario M1P 3E6
Tel: 800 387 5167
www.estelledesigns.ca

Koigu Wool Designs
Box 158
Chatsworth, Ontario N0H 1G0
Tel: 888 765 WOOL
www.koigu.com

Patons
320 Livingstone Avenue South
PO Box 40
Listowel ON N4W 3H3
Tel: 888 368 8401
www.patonsyarns.com

EUROPE

BC Garn
BC Garn Aps,
Albuen 56A
6000 Kolding§
Denmark
Tel: 0045 75 89 73 84
www.bcgarn.dk

GGH
Mühlenstraße 74
D-25421 Pinneberg
Germany
Tel: 0049 (0)4101 208484
www.ggh-garn.com

Lang Yarns
Mühlehofstrasse 9
6260 Reiden
Switzerland
Tel: 0041 (0)62 749 01 11

Lang Garn and Wollen GmbH
Puellenweg 20
41352 Korschenbroich
Germany
Tel: 0049 (0)2161 574 910
www.langyarns.com

Index

Figures in italics indicate captions.

Acknowledgements

Author's Acknowledgements

This is a book that I have had in my mind in some form or other for many, many years and has been a long time in the making. It would simply not have been possible to get it finished without the help of some very special people. I have to send out my eternal gratitude to Patricia, Tarina, Mhairi, Jean, Julia, Bekki and Vanessa, who are all incredibly accomplished knitters, thanks for your tips, advice and encouragement. Special thanks also to my friends Clare, Cheryl, Patsy and Mary who helped out with those critical extra pieces of knitting when it all became too much for my little hands to cope with.

The team who have worked on the book have been great; thanks to the design team and Lisa and Lucy for their support.

I am extremely grateful to the yarn companies who donated yarn, especially to the lovely Eva from Shilasdair and Jenni from Fyberspates who dyed yarn especially for the book.

Finally, to Sean and my family, thanks as always. They have been an incredible support throughout the many ups and downs of writing a book, dealing with AWOL yarn and rows of more than 400 stitches! A heartfelt thanks to you all,

Claire

Picture Credits

The publishers would like to thank the following sources for their kind permission to reproduce the pictures in this book.

Key: t=Top, b=Bottom, c=Centre, l=Left and r=Right

The Advertising Archives (Image Courtesy of): 35, 36tr (Evening dresses magazine plate), 81, 82bl (Blue sweater with button detail), 125br (Models wearing ponchos) **Alamy:** /Wonderstock: 140 **The Bridgeman Art Library:** /Deutsches Tapetenmuseum, Kassel, Germany /© Museumslandschaft Hessen Kassel Gabriele Boessert, Rose wallpaper design by Ludwig Raubenheimer, produced by H. Stranven, Bonn c.1925 (wallpaper), German School, (20th century): 12 **Corbis:** /Blue Lantern Studio: 16-17b (Magazine fashion illustration by Brauer), /Condé Nast Archive: 17t (Two women with a telescope), 34, 56, 80, 100, 101, 102ct (Model wearing orange headband), 103cb (Models posing with cars), 123, 142, /Elisa Lazo de Valdez: 16t (Girl in fringed dress), /Ross Marino/Sygma: 144bl (Madonna), /© Sie Producations: 15 **Jules Dohmen:** /www.snufver.deviantart.com: 76-77 (background), 163 (background) **Getty:** /FPG: 124bl (1970s Tea party), /Hulton Archive: 36br (Loretta Young), 122, /Popperfoto: 58t (Winding wartime wool), 103tr (Models in hot pink & tangerine sweaters), /Time & Life Pictures: 59br (Women in tea dresses) **Mary Evans Picture Library:** /Illustrated London News Ltd: 14, /Anthony Lipmann: 37tr (Dryden watercolour, orange top and green beret), /National Magazine Company: 57, /Adrian Woodhouse: 83cl (Beige-green Victor Stiebel suit), 83tr (Pink Victor Stiebel suit) **Patricia Roberts Designs (Copyright, All Rights Reserved):** 124br (Rose Petal © 1979), 125tl (Plain Dealing © 1975), 144br (Columbine © 1980), 145tl (Calamity © 1980) **Picture Desk:** /Kobal Colllection/Paramount: 16b (The Great Gatsby), 145cr (Flashdance) **Rex Features:** /Argenpress: 58br (Modelling Over the Knee Socks), /Krakstrom: 124tr (Models eating ice lollies), /Sipa Press: 143, /Bill Zygmant: 102b (Models wearing mini dresses) **Victoria & Albert Museum/V&A Images:** 78, 98, 120

www.the-banana-lounge.com: 113, 117, 130, 132 (Background)

Every effort has been made to acknowledge correctly and contact the source and/or copyright holder of each picture and Carlton Books Limited apologizes for any unintentional errors or omissions, which will be, corrected in future editions of this book.

Publisher's Acknowledgements

We would like to thank the following suppliers and sources for contributing to the book.

Vintage clothes loaned by:

Vintage Modes
Grays Antique Market
1–7 Davies Mews
London W1K 5AB
Tel: 020 7409 0400
www.vintagemodes.co.uk

This Shop Rocks
131 Brick Lane
London E1 6SE
Tel: 020 7739 7667

Vintage Store London
182 Brick Lane
London E1 6SA
www.thevintagestorelondon.co.uk

Vintage costume jewellery loaned by:

Linda Bee
Stand M10-M12
Grays Antique Market
1–7 Davies Mews
London W1K 5AB
Tel: 020 7629 5921

Gillian Horsup
Grays Antique Market
1–7 Davies Mews
London W1K 5AB
Tel: 020 7499 8121
www.gillianhorsup.com

The antique chair on cover shot was kindly loaned by Caroline Molloy.